New Intelligence for a Smarter Planet

Driving Business Innovation with IBM Analytic Solutions

Pat Bates
Mike Biere
Rex Wiederanders
Alan Meyer
Bill Wong

MC Press Online, LP
Lewisville, TX 75077

New Intelligence for a Smarter Planet
Driving Business Innovation with IBM Analytic Solutions
Pat Bates, Mike Biere, Rex Wiederanders, Alan Meyer, Bill Wong

First Printing—October 2009

MC Press offers excellent discounts on this book when ordered in quantity for bulk purchases or special sales, which may include custom covers and content particular to your business, training goals, marketing focus, and/or branding interest.

For information regarding permissions or special orders, please contact:
MC Press
Corporate Offices
125 N. Woodland Trail
Lewisville, TX 75077 USA

For information regarding sales and/or customer service, please contact:
MC Press
P.O. Box 4300
Big Sandy, TX 75755-4300 USA

ISBN: 978-158347-086-2

About the Authors

Pat Bates is a senior member of the Worldwide Technical Sales Enablement group focusing on data warehousing and analytics software technologies. Pat has worked in this space for the past 15 years, including the past 8 years at IBM in roles ranging from software development, management, product management and technical sales enablement. Pat has spoken frequently at industry conferences and has contributed to several papers and articles in the areas of data warehousing and business intelligence.

Mike Biere is a senior member of IBM's Worldwide Team for Data Warehousing and Business Intelligence. He had held numerous positions within IBM as a technical specialist in database, data warehousing, and business intelligence since 1978. He has had three separate IBM careers with sints on the outside as a data warehouse / business intelligence consultant and a Director of Product Management for Cognos. He is a frequent presenter/speaker at events such as IDUG and is a published author, *Business Intelligence for the Enterprise*.

Alan Meyer is the Marketing Manager for Data Warehousing in IBM's InfoSphere organization. Alan has been involved in the BI community since the mid 1980s and has held both technical and marketing positions in data warehousing and business intelligence. His prior experiences covers a broad spectrum from hardware maintenance, application programming, systems programming and consulting. He has been a frequent speaker at industry events and has written numerous papers and articles on topics of innovating with information and holds several software patents.

Rex Wiederanders is the manager of the Worldwide Technical Sales Enablement group, of which he has been a member for 12 years. Rex has held various positions in

IBM since 1981, including sales, technical sales, development, and above region specialties. Concentrating on software for the past 20 years, Rex has been a frequent speaker at many trade shows and user groups, where his unique presentation style has been well-received.

Bill Wong is an Information Management executive responsible for delivering information-led transformation solutions. He has supported IBM database and data warehouse offerings since their inception, held roles in development, marketing, and sales, and has spent several years assisting companies implement solutions in the financial services, retail, and telecommunications industries. He is a frequent speaker at industry events, and his previous books have focused on database technology, business intelligence solutions in the life sciences industry, and how to drive business optimization with trusted information.

Acknowledgements

We would to thank and acknowledge the following people for their support, guidance, and contributions on this primer:

Kevin Sy, Aliye Ergulen, Catherine Haddad, Gary O'Connell, Stephanie Best, Natasha Engan, Susan Visser, Rick Miller, Lynn Jonas, Stephanie Clark, Drew Friedrich, Caryn Meyers, Meg Dussault, Guenter Sauter, John Rollins, Adam Gartenberg, Bill O'Connell, Karl Freund, Maria Winans, Inhi Cho, Greg Lotko, Arvind Krishna, Ambuj Goyal, and Steve Mills

Contents

Foreword

Welcome and thank you for taking time to understand the IBM Smarter Planet initiative, focused on New Intelligence.

The world we live in today is increasingly instrumented, interconnected, and intelligent. We are experiencing a revolution, and information is at the heart of it. Businesses that are taking advantage of this new wealth of information are able to make more intelligent decisions and are rising to the top. They are managing large volumes of information in real-time, incorporating analytics and predictive modeling, pervasively collecting and sharing information across the entire value chain, and speeding time to value by delivering trusted, accurate and timely information to the right decision makers. In short, they're discovering a new kind of intelligence.

Today's smart businesses are no longer content to look back, but are using this wealth of information to look forward. New intelligence goes beyond providing a view of your current operations, and provides a glimpse at the future.

It provides a likely view of what is just around the corner and even further down the road. Analytics and reporting tools slice and dice data, crystallizing trends, patterns and anomalies that yield invaluable business insights to help you drive smarter decision-making.

IBM is committed to your success and we have assembled our best subject matter experts to deliver this introductory primer to help guide you and support your information-led transformation efforts.

Arvind Krishna

Arvind Krishna
General Manager, Information Management
IBM Software Group

1

Introducing the Smarter Planet

Leaders from around the world are focused more than ever on the economic, social, and environmental implications of global integration, where free-trade agreements, the Internet, and globalization are making the world simultaneously smaller, flatter, and smarter. Something that may ultimately have a more profound affect on our society, businesses, and individual lives—the planet is also becoming smarter. The IBM Smart Planet initiative concentrates on the world's infrastructure, those systems and processes that enable goods to be developed, manufactured, bought and sold, and services that deliver everything from electricity and financial transactions, to efficient healthcare—to name a few—and that directly affect billions of lives.

The world's infrastructure is becoming "smart." Consider the following:

- There are more than 1 billion transistors per human

- An estimated 2 billion people will soon be on the Internet

- At the same time, we are heading toward one trillion connected objects—comprising "the Internet of things"

- Worldwide mobile telephone subscriptions has surpassed 3.3 billion—one for every two people on the planet

- Over 30 billion Radio Frequency Identification (RFID) tags are produced globally, embedded in products, passports, buildings—even animals

- Hundreds of satellites are in orbit around the Earth, generating terabytes of data every day

And it's not just about pervasive connectivity. For the first time, massively powerful computers can be affordably applied to processing, modeling, forecasting, and analyzing just about any workload or task. *Cloud computing* is emerging as a means to connect and provision the proliferating array of end-user devices, sensors, and actuators with powerful, massively scaleable back-end systems. The PC model of the 1980s has been replaced by a new paradigm, based on openness, networks, powerful new technology, and the integration of digital intelligence into the fabric of everyday work and life.

As these systems become smarter, they will increasingly exhibit three distinct characteristics (Fig. 1.1). They will be:

- *Instrumented*: Any activity or process can now be measured, better understood, modeled, and improved upon to generate valuable new insight.

- *Interconnected*: By tapping into the collective intelligence of the entire value chain through the connection of whole systems, the world can become more highly self-regulated, optimized, and efficient.

- *Intelligent*: Every insight derived from this world of smart devices can lead to incremental value by enabling actions to be handled more automatically and with far greater certainty.

Organizations will now be able to make faster, better-informed decisions to drive smarter business outcomes because their systems can be made *instrumented, interconnected,* and *intelligent.*

INSTRUMENTED	INTERCONNECTED	INTELLIGENT
We now have the ability to measure, sense and monitor the condition of almost everything.	People, systems and objects can communicate and interact with each other in entirely new ways.	We can respond to changes quickly and accurately, and get better results by predicting and optimizing for future events.

Figure 1.1: The world is becoming increasingly instrumented, interconnected, and intelligent

For the first time in history, almost anything can become digitally aware and interconnected. The planet is becoming more intelligent, more instrumented, and more interconnected day by day. And with these changes come amazing opportunities for society as a whole and for every business, institution, and individual. With so much technology and networking abundantly available, what wouldn't you put smart technology into? What service wouldn't you provide? What wouldn't you connect? What information wouldn't you mine for insight?

The answer is, "There's nothing you can't do." With modern technology, you—or your competitor—will do it all. You will do it because you can. But the even more compelling reason we will all begin to transform our systems, operations, enterprises and personal lives to take advantage of a smarter world isn't just because we can. It's because we must.

In the Smarter Planet, businesses do three things well (Fig. 1.2):

- *Focus on value*: Smart companies do more with less, focus on their core business initiatives, and exploit their relationships to ensure financial solidity while continually revisiting and revalidating their core objectives to remain flexible enough to grow with their customers.

- *Exploit opportunities:* Smart companies know how to capture share in their market, build future capabilities by protecting and acquiring talent, and are the top performers in their industries, making bold moves where required.

- *Act with speed*: Smart companies have leaders who get the information required to act, set, and communicate the organization's agenda, and empower their line of business leaders to manage change and move quickly.

Figure 1.2: Smarter organizations must focus on value, opportunity, and speed

Understanding the Smarter Planet

In this new world, as every human being, company, organization, city, nation, natural system, and man-made system becomes interconnected, instrumented, and literally made more intelligent, we believe the following questions must be considered (Fig. 1.3).

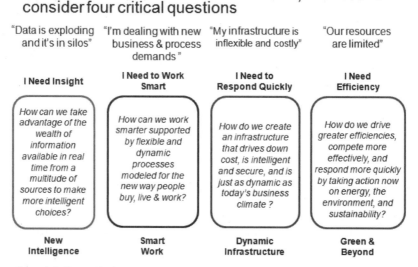

Figure 1.3: Four critical questions that drive business

Let's discuss each of these issues in more detail. Why are they important? What are the pressures we face? Where can we look for solutions? How have enterprises already been working on smart solutions to their problems?

New Intelligence

Smart Businesses are taking advantage of the wealth of information available to make more intelligent decisions. New intelligence solutions deliver value across one or more of the following dimensions:

- *Information management*: Effective management and use of the explosive volume and variety of historical and real-time information

- *Predictive capability*: Identifying and proactively addressing opportunities and threats with predictive analytics in real time

- *Engaging the value chain*: Pervasive information, collected from a multitude of sources across the value chain and made useful to all who need it

- *Operating with speed*: Speeding time to value by delivering trusted, accurate, and timely information to the right decision makers at all levels within the organization

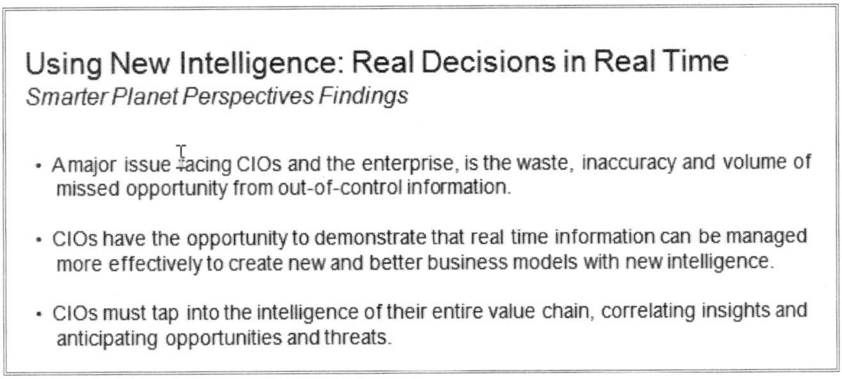

Using New Intelligence: Real Decisions in Real Time
Smarter Planet Perspectives Findings

- A major issue facing CIOs and the enterprise, is the waste, inaccuracy and volume of missed opportunity from out-of-control information.

- CIOs have the opportunity to demonstrate that real time information can be managed more effectively to create new and better business models with new intelligence.

- CIOs must tap into the intelligence of their entire value chain, correlating insights and anticipating opportunities and threats.

Figure 1.4: New Intelligence issues

Smart Work

Smart work is about applying new levels of intelligence to how every person, organization, and man-made system interacts. Each interaction represents a chance to do things better, more efficiently, and productively through agile, flexible business models.

Increasingly, businesses rely upon employees, customers, partners, and suppliers to collaborate and interact more effectively. Processes need to adapt dynamically to changing economic conditions to mitigate risk and drive profit. The foundational components for a smarter planet already exist, and smart work is a reality today.

Key attributes of smart work are:

- *Agile business models* help businesses quickly shift direction to reflect economic realities.

- *Collaboration* helps people extend internal and external relationships to expand expertise and access new information and resources outside their usual workgroups.

- *Dynamic business processes* help businesses access trusted information, reuse assets, and reduce costs by automating manual processes.

- *Smart Service Oriented Architecture* (SOA) converts siloed, inefficient applications into reusable services.

Smart Work: Embrace Change, Empower People, Drive Profit
Smarter Planet Perspectives Findings

- Organizations that are supported by flexible business models, dynamic business processes, and collaborative work environments will be uniquely positioned to win.

- Reaching the new connected customer takes personalization, co-creation and a combination of business and IT skills.

- These attributes will allow companies to provide a rich user experience to customers, suppliers, employees and partners.

- The ability to work smarter and adapt to changing economic conditions are critical to mitigating risk and driving profit.

Figure 1.5: Smart work

Dynamic Infrastructure

A dynamic infrastructure is designed to help transform physical and digital assets into more valued services. A dynamic infrastructure is highly optimized to achieve greater results with improved management, and to leverages new technologies and strategies to reduce costs and deliver superior business and IT services with agility and speed.

A dynamic infrastructure can deliver three distinct benefits across the entire organization while also laying the foundation for the future:

- *Improve service*: Internal and external customers and employees expect superior service—not only regarding the high availability and quality of existing services, but also to meet their rising expectations for real-time, dynamic access to innovative new services.

- *Reduce cost*: Bottom-line cost reduction is important, but a dynamic infrastructure can also help achieve breakthroughs in productivity gains through virtualization, optimization, energy stewardship, and flexible sourcing.

- *Manage risk*: Security, resiliency, and compliance are already expectations in today's environment. Dynamic organizations need to prepare for the new risks posed by an even more connected and collaborative world.

Secure, Resilient, Smart: Leveraging Dynamic Infrastructure for Business Innovation
Smarter Planet Perspectives Findings

- CIOs understand that to realize the potential of a smarter planet, sooner rather than later their businesses will have to rethink their IT infrastructure and begin to modernize on quite a large scale.

- With any kind of restoration, there are pitfalls – like the tendency to invest in what we have instead of what we need.

- What can CIOs do to extend the life of current infrastructure while establishing a foundation for building out a stronger infrastructure that enables future innovation and growth.

Figure 1.6: Dynamic infrastructure

Green & Beyond

The environment is a pervasive and urgent issue for the public, with pressure building from government agencies and other key influencers for increased accountability in areas that impact the environment and society. The business of becoming more "green" needs to be good for the business as well as for the environment. Private enterprises, public organizations, communities, regions, and entire industries are faced with developing strategies and solutions for becoming more environmentally responsible in ways that also generate new revenue opportunities and lower costs and risk. Rising energy costs and environmental compliance and governance mandates are pushing CIOs and data centers to a tipping point, requiring new strategies and infrastructure; IT has the mandate to use "green" as an umbrella for broader transformation.

Intelligent energy and carbon management improvements are about adding intelligence to passive or "dumb" systems to create "smart systems" that are dramatically more efficient and reliable, and therefore enabled to save energy and resources. Intelligent utility networks, transportation systems, and oilfields will all become more efficient. These are real solutions, available today, that harness and leverage the power of built-in intelligence to:

- Improve energy management

- Make our energy have less impact to the environment and be more reliable

- Reduce traffic congestion and associated greenhouse gas emissions

- Reduce energy demand

Green and Beyond: Smart Environmental Strategies for Competitive Advantage
Smarter Planet Perspectives Findings

- CIOs can help their organizations find the value in green – value that includes cost efficiencies and optimized business processes to reduce the cost of operations, lower their company's environmental impact and improve productivity.

- Facing the challenge of taming the rapid increase in data center energy consumption, CIOs must evaluate and extend existing IT investments and deploy more efficient future IT infrastructure – with better controls, lower cost and less impact.

- CIOs have the opportunity to capitalize on the emergence of smart systems that will have a profound effect on challenges facing the planet.

- Greater insight and energy savings across the business can be achieved by adding intelligence to passive or "dumb" systems - creating new smarter systems that are dramatically more efficient and reliable.

Figure 1.7: Green & beyond

Why New Intelligence Now? Why Today?

Enterprises are handling more information than ever before, yet know they are not keeping pace.

- A foremost issue facing enterprises today is the waste, inaccuracy, and volume of missed opportunities that stem from the single root cause of information raging out of control.

- At the same time, almost anything can now become digitally aware and interconnected, from our roads to our appliances to our clothing. Technology and networking is abundantly available at low cost, bringing major implications for the value that can be derived from interconnected instruments.

- The danger stemming from more information coming from more devices is increased complexity. Organizations that can decipher and predict emerging trends will gain competitive advantage.

- Competitive advantage is hard to sustain when based solely on gains in productivity and cost efficiency in transactional work—simple automation is just table stakes and provides no competitive differentiation.

Business Challenges

Volume

Every day, 15 petabytes of new information are generated. It is estimated that the codified information base of the world is now doubling every 11 hours.

Variety

80% of new data growth is unstructured content, generated largely by email, with increasing contribution by documents, images, video and audio.

Velocity

A company with 1,000 employees spends $5.3 million a year to find information stored on its servers. 42% of managers say they use the wrong information at least once per week.

Figure 1.8: The challenges of New Intelligence

New Intelligence brings together the power of human cognition and computational excellence. It shifts the agenda to situational awareness and *prediction.* This drives focus toward *optimization*—for example, shifts from reactive public safety to proactive crime prevention, from disease monitoring and management to epidemic prediction and prevention, from decision support to decision delegation, and ultimately to predictive capability as the surest path to move beyond traditional notions of "sense and respond." The new reality of the world we are entering is that, if you're responding, it might already be too late. In effect, a world that is flat, fast, pressurized, and volatile drives a requirement *to be both fast, and right.*

New Intelligence is giving smarter organizations entirely new capabilities for optimizing business processes, collaborating and driving innovation.

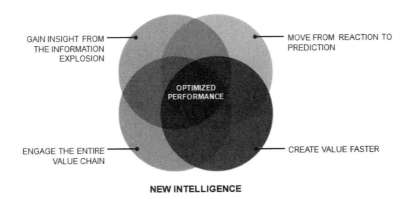

Figure 1.9: The opportunities of New Intelligence

Discovering New Intelligence

More and more information is available, but proportionally less of it—and radically less of the information being created in real-time—is being effectively captured, managed, analyzed, and made available to people who need it. We are crossing a new threshold in our ability to capture, process, model, evaluate, aggregate, prioritize, forecast, and analyze how the world's major economic, social, and physical systems work in fundamentally new and deeper ways. To effectively harness that ability in our organizations, an intelligent, robust information infrastructure is needed.

To cope with this explosion of data, creating new data centers with exponentially larger storage and faster processing is necessary, but by itself is not sufficient. The flow of information must be managed to deliver richer insights and to make faster, better decisions. New intelligence applications enable the transformation of information into a strategic asset that can be rapidly leveraged for sustained competitive advantage.

To keep up with ever-shortening cycle times, more and more decisions must be pushed down in the organization, requiring many more people to have *real-time* access to much deeper insights. Even with more advanced tools to systematically mine new structured and unstructured data, and to collaborate on sharing insights and decision making, we will still reach the limits of human capacity. New intelligence will demand that more and more real-time operating decisions be linked to the systems themselves (inventory, flows, hedging). This information from markets, supply chains, customers, and smart devices creates instant reaction and proactive action in this smarter world.

An information-led transformation is a journey that can begin—and deliver immediate value—at any stage in an organization's maturity in its use of information. It does not require major investments of resources or time to deliver value. And you can start at any point, depending on where you are in your own journey. But to capture the full value of an information-led transformation, you must look at all three elements:

- *Plan your information strategy*: You must ensure that you have a plan to align your information with your business objectives, including understanding how information can best be applied in situations that may be unique to your industry or field.

- *Apply business analytics to optimize decisions*: You must be able to make better, faster, more accurate decisions through planning, monitoring, reporting, and analysis of your information.

- *Establish a flexible information platform*: You must have the necessary technology platform and infrastructure to support your needs and to ensure that information can serve as a trusted asset that can be shared and securely accessed by all who need it, when and where they need it.

Whether you start by first planning a strategy, improving the underlying infrastructure, or addressing a specific business need, or with tactical changes, it is possible to see improvements in business optimization—with tangible return on investment (ROI)—from the onset. At the same time, you can lay a foundation and a standard set of information services that can be leveraged more readily in the future. These elements will be discussed further in the following chapters.

2

New Intelligence
Business Analytics Overview

The emergence of a global economy is forcing organizations to seek to become more nimble with their operations and more innovative with their decisions. In the face of exploding data volumes and shrinking batch-time windows, these organizations are struggling to make real-time or near-real-time decisions and thereby gain competitive advantage.

Valuable information comes in many forms, from structured to unstructured, operational to transactional, real-time to historical; it is scattered throughout every enterprise. This information may reside in databases and data warehouses, e-mails and transaction logs, customer call logs, shopper behavior or repair orders, or it may be XML data locked up inside transactional systems that cannot be used or analyzed in databases.

If this data can be unleashed and leveraged properly, however, then businesses can make better decisions to drive sales, improve processes and services, boost team productivity, reduce the risks inherent in doing business, and streamline relationships with customers, trading partners, and suppliers.

The Smarter Planet allows companies to focus on value, exploit opportunities, and act with speed. But how does one gain these admirable goals, and how difficult is it to build a system that is instrumented, interconnected, and intelligent? We will examine how to implement such a system later in Chapter 4, but here we will take a close look at the brain of a Smart Analytic System and how business users go about their day and benefit from the enormous capability of such a system.

The brain of an analytic system is, of course, the analytics. But analytics is not contained within one piece of software, one subsystem, or a database. Analytics is the combination of myriad processes (predictive and descriptive modeling, optimization, data preparation) running within the warehouse to extract essential information in the context of business discovery and business process modeling, the warehouse itself (platform, functionalities), the desktop reporting and analysis tooling (implementation, deployment to business users), and, too rarely mentioned, the minds of the people using the system to derive greater business value from the analytic system. Thus, gray matter meets glass, analytic/algorithmic processes, and warehouse.

For the rest of this chapter, we will consider the hierarchy of analytical layers depicted in Figure 2.1, where end-user tooling is supported by various analytic processes that are in turn supported by IBM systems for warehousing and analytic acceleration. This hierarchy consists of a user interface layer (end-user tooling), an analytic process layer (system processes and algorithms for analytics), and an infrastructure layer (warehousing and Smart Analytics components).

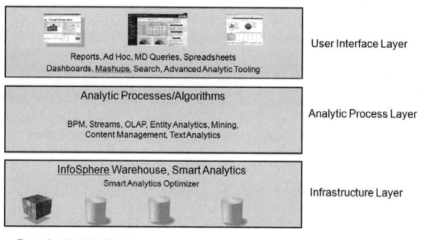

Figure 2.1: Analytical layers

A successful Smart Analytics System will answer four questions for the business user. The answer to each question represents greater value and return on investment. The end-user tooling and analytic processes vary by question, while the warehousing infrastructure provides the centralized foundation for all of the tooling and analytics.

How is my business performing? The business user looks at prepared reports and interprets the results. The end-user tools most often used are standard prepared reports but may include ad hoc reporting as well. The underlying analytic processes are primarily standard or interactive query but could also incorporate standardized results from advanced analytics (e.g., data mining) as well.

Why is my business performing this way? In this case, the user is often doing his own calculations, going beyond what has been built into standard reports, looking for deeper understanding of the contributors to business results. The tools used are often spreadsheets, ad hoc reporting, and multidimensional (MD) analysis. Analytic processes generally include interactive query and online analytical processing (OLAP) and may also utilize standardized or ad hoc results derived from prebuilt data mining models.

What would happen to my business results if I make a particular change? These users are looking to reduce expenses and/or increase revenue, often with no organizational changes to the business. An example would be to predict an increase in profit based on a projected increase in sales resulting from a marketing campaign. The tools used are usually spreadsheets and graphical user interfaces with MD analysis and data mining capabilities. Analytic processes may include some combination of query, OLAP, and ad hoc results from data mining models, including "on the fly" execution of prespecified or "guided" mining processes.

How can I best change my business model to gain further competitive advantage? The highest-value scenario, this type of questioning is used to determine how behavioral and organizational changes will impact the profitability of the business. To answer these questions, several tools are typically employed. Each of these tools exercises advanced analytic processes and algorithms within the warehouse. Examples of these processes are OLAP, data mining, and text analytics, generally requiring high-level analytical skills. The processes may rely upon historical data, forecast data, point of sale data, unstructured data, and third-party data such as demographics and credit history.

A note about Extensible Markup Language (XML)

Over the last few years, XML has become the de facto standard for exchange of information between organizations, as well as between departments or applications within the same organization. With its inherent flexibility and extensibility, XML is proving to be an ideal means for modeling semistructured and frequently changing business information, as well as a standard for exchanging information through web services. Its useful applications range from common business document interchange to very specialized domains such as life sciences.

Recognizing the power and popularity of XML, and therefore its value to business analytics and New Intelligence, IBM has led the industry in native XML support. IBM Information Management and Analytics software manages and operates over XML data as a first-class structure, native to the engines and processes—not as an add-on extension. As XML has become as fundamental to business analytics as traditional relations data has always been, IBM made support for XML intrinsic to everything from mashups, search, and data mining, to content management and text analytics.

End User Interaction with Information

End users employ many tools to gain insights from the analytic system. For each tool or approach, we explain how the tool is used and what business insight is derived.

Reports

Many kinds of reports exist, but the most common is the scheduled report, often in "greenbar" format as illustrated in Figure 2.2. The user can request Information Services to have changes made to the report, but for the most part the report remains the same week after week. As a rule, a great deal of thought goes into the creation of such a report, and many processes are run in batch to achieve the results. These reports have broad business value, and users know how to flip to the correct page to locate their information. Once there, the user will often need to do further study or perform additional calculations to better understand the business results. (Hardcopy reports marked up with derived values are a common sight at most companies.) Standard reports are usually distributed online, and the report may have a feature that allows the user to export the data to a spreadsheet. Lacking that function, users may employ screen scrapers, copy and paste, and, sadly, retyping of data into that universal analysis tool: the spreadsheet.

Product ID	Product Name	Units In Stock	Units On Order	Reorder Level
101	Frozen Peas	147	200	150
1571	Snuggles	15	10	20
1362	Digital Clock	4	10	5
400054	Odor Eaters	35	50	25
821	Bic Click	101	0	75
3347	DB2 For Dummies	1527	1500	2000

Figure 2.2: Greenbar report

The report example in Figure 2.2 illustrates how a particular portion of a report may not contain all the information that a user needs (e.g., no information on sales). Sales information may be listed in another area in the report, requiring the user to tab through the report and jot down values to build an understanding of the business situation.

The great business value of the standard report is that it can serve a large number of users and provide a large number of answers to many diverse questions. The bad news is that one must know the report well to find pertinent data, and the report itself does nothing to help the user derive the new information. For instance, Profit can be calculated by subtracting Total Expenses from Total Sales, but one must search out, calculate, and format the values. Standard reports can be enhanced with visually appealing tabular data, graphics, and charts, as illustrated in Figure 2.3.

Figure 2.3: Cognos reporting with graphics and charting

As opposed to greenbar reports, graphical reports are usually built for a specific department and a specific business problem. These are still canned reports, but they offer a much-improved format for understanding the data. Most even include a limited drill-down capability, with charts that react to changes. Users of these reports can quickly determine how their business is operating, and to varying degrees, perform further analysis into why the business is performing as it is.

Ad Hoc Reports

When a user decides that a special report is needed, usually for a single, one-time purpose, he can either calculate the new report from a standard report, or issue his own query for just the data needed using an ad hoc report. We all love to know the deeper meanings of things, and ad hoc comes from the Latin, meaning "for this purpose." It is common to have users collect many ad hoc report templates and just tweak a few settings to get a new report.

When a user is doing his work and is looking to determine how the business is performing, we can see that he has several ways to come up with answers. The data may be in a standard report, derived from a standard report, or produced with a new or modified ad hoc report. There is no way to make a blanket statement about which is the best method, for the answer depends on the complexity of the calculation and the degree to which the result can be calculated from standard and ad hoc reports.

Most graphical tools for ad hoc analysis are easy to use and rather intuitive, allowing users to build quick snapshots of those areas of the business they wish to examine. The outputs of Cognos tooling are spectacular and provide rich formatting and charting capability, as illustrated in Figure 2.4.

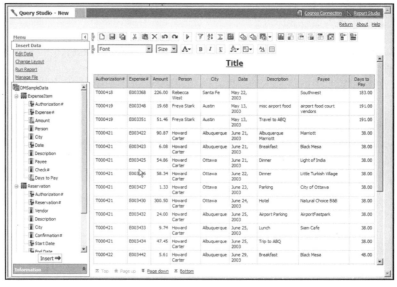

Figure 2.4: Cognos tooling for ad hoc analysis

Taken together, standard reports and ad hoc analysis can provide a great deal of analytical capability that some users need. This capability is limited to questions around "How is my business performing?" and does not readily address "Why is my business performing this way?" The user must drill deeper into the business data to follow the trail of information to answer the latter question. Reports and ad hoc reporting do not lend themselves to answering these questions, so user communities have moved to using spreadsheets, often populated by data copied from reports and ad hoc queries.

Spreadsheets

A great many of the "how and why" questions can be addressed by using macros, pivot tables, and charting within spreadsheets. As previously mentioned, users have developed many methods to load spreadsheets, and a subset of users have become quite good at analyzing the data within spreadsheets. The problem has become one of interconnection and intelligence; that is, warehouse data and the spreadsheet are not connected, and the only intelligence is contained within the spreadsheet macros.

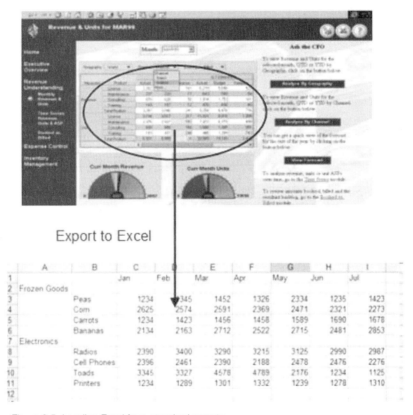

Figure 2.5: Loading Excel from standard reports

At first glance, one would wonder why a user would ever move data from a graphical report to a spreadsheet. And, if that was all the user was doing, almost everyone would agree that this is a bad idea. Since the introduction of the electronic spreadsheet, users have been combining data from multiple sources into one view, and using their own calculations, to derive new business insight.

Multidimensional Analysis

MD analysis is a common method of determining business behavior, but the term has many meanings and its roots go way back to early programming. In the late 1960s, IBM introduced A Programming Language (APL), which has a rich set of arcane but powerful MD variables and operators. Most of the world ignored APL, but MD analysis saw its resurgence when the spreadsheet became popular. So, just what is MD analysis?

MD has become accepted to mean the calculation of one business measurement (e.g., sales, margin, profit, expense) against many other dimensions, such as time, product, and location. The succinct expression is usually something like: "What is my Profit by Time, by Customer, by Product, by Distribution Channel?" Each "by" adds an additional dimension of thought, making the above example a four-dimensional query; Business Measure, Time, Product, and Distribution Channel.

Each dimension has a natural hierarchy built to reflect how the company does its business, and how the analyst understands that dimension. The best way to understand a dimensional hierarchy is to look at time, which might have a hierarchy of Year, Quarter, Month, Week, and Day. The analyst may be looking at the Month level, but can easily move up to the Quarter level or down to the Week level. In the next example, the analyst has defined five dimensions in Excel. The Product dimension is nested within the Business Measurements dimension, and Time and Actual/Budget are nested. Each dimension is shown at some level or levels in its hierarchy; Products are shown at two levels.

	A	B	C	D	E	F	G	H	I	J
1						Region 1				
2			Jan		Feb		Mar		Qtr1	
3			Actual	Budget	Actual	Budget	Actual	Budget	Actual	Budget
4	Vests	Sales	1812	1690	1754	1640	1805	1690	5371	5020
5		Costs	599	550	588	540	596	540	1783	1630
6		Margin	1213	1140	1166	1100	1209	1150	3588	3390
7		Profit	837	860	792	820	832	870	2461	2550
8	Pullovers	Sales	200	190	206	190	214	200	620	580
9		Costs	84	80	86	80	89	80	259	240
10		Margin	116	110	120	110	125	120	361	340
11		Profit	67	70	71	70	74	80	212	220
12	Cardigans	Sales	93	80	101	90	107	100	301	270
13		Costs	38	30	41	30	43	40	122	100
14		Margin	55	50	60	60	64	60	179	170
15		Profit	20	30	25	40	29	40	74	110
16	Sweaters	Sales	2105	1960	2061	1920	2126	1990	6292	5870
17		Costs	721	660	715	650	728	660	2164	1970
18		Margin	1384	1300	1346	1270	1398	1330	4128	3900
19		Profit	924	960	888	930	935	990	2747	2880
20										

Figure 2.6: Excel example of multidimensional analysis

The power of MD analysis lies in the analyst's ability to drill up and down within each dimension, and pivot dimensions around to gain understanding from the information.

Since the introduction of Visicalc in the early 1980s, consumers of data have happily adopted the spreadsheet as the tool of choice for their own analysis, and MD analysis is the most frequently used format.

Analysts chose to move to spreadsheets because standard reporting methods could not supply the information they needed. They needed to analyze data, and drill up and down through business hierarchies on their own business terms. To do this, they performed their own extract, transform, and load (ETL) operations from multiple sources—usually the reports they had in hand—augmented by data from transaction and warehouse databases. The analytic calculations they did right within the spreadsheet, using macros and spreadsheet aggregations. Each spreadsheet can be considered a small datamart, with its accompanying ETL and imbedded analytics.

It is not unusual to find finance departments tracking 10,000 spreadsheets for their businesses. Taken from a broader business point of view, this is a disaster—thousands to tens of thousands of datamarts, undocumented ETL processes, and analytical calculations unique to each analyst. Little wonder then that one of the most common complaints among analysts is that everyone has different numbers, and everyone thinks his are correct.

As we see in Figure 2.7, MD analysis tooling can be quite elegant with the addition of graphics and charting. Cognos allows slicing and dicing of the data with synchronized charts.

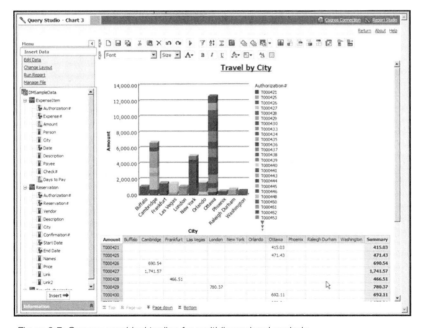

Figure 2.7: Cognos graphical tooling for multidimensional analysis

The rapid emergence and maturation of web- and services-based technologies provide key capabilities in the analytics framework to meet the rising demands for new intelligence. Highly dynamic, adaptive, personalized, and social networking technologies such as dashboards, Web 2.0-enabled mashups, and enterprise search combine to empower more interconnected end-user decision-makers with the enriched information they need to accelerate intelligent decisions. Here, we examine these new-generation graphical tools.

Dashboards

Dashboards, whether deployed corporate-wide or highly customized for a single group, or even a single user, have emerged as an information industry standard starting point from which almost all other analytic activity is launched. They have become the essential "home page," the first thing a knowledge worker sees at the start of her day, and the instrument she monitors throughout her business day. And indeed, with the advances of pervasive delivery on virtually any mobile device or channel, dashboards are available and accessible 24/7, anytime, anywhere.

Simply speaking, an analytic dashboard, along with its close cousin the *scorecard*, provides a concise, interactive, densely graphical, single-screen view of key performance indicators and critical up-to-the-minute business information. Integrated into the analytics framework, the dashboard collates key information, in the context both of the business role of the end user consuming the information, and of the business process that user is performing. Not simply an information provider, the dashboard also enables the user to take action, through interactive links and navigation. An example is shown in Figure 2.8.

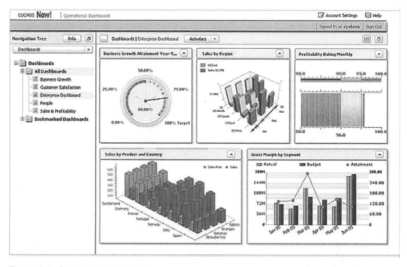

Figure 2.8: Dashboard example

Individual dashboards will naturally vary greatly, but all share typical characteristics:

- *Multiple sources of information in context*: To be useful, dashboards bring together a variety of information and analytics from different sources into a single concise view, both in context of the business requirements they are meant to address, and also in context to each other. These sources may be internal and external to the organization.

- *Pervasive access to analytics*: Dashboards provide interconnectivity between end users and the analytics framework by providing access points to the full range of assets and applications. Everything from a simple canned report to a network of linked OLAP cubes to advanced predictive and data mining functions can be exposed in a manner and context easily consumed by the business user. Dashboards provide a consistent user experience regardless of the content or the complex processes behind the screen. Primarily web-based, dashboards deliver analytics to a world of end users on the tool they use the most—their web browser.

- *Interactive and linked*: To go beyond passive snapshots of information, dashboards must be highly interactive and linked. Performance monitors and indicators are hot-linked to take users, in one click, to more detailed reports, applications, or business processes. Information representations on a dashboard are also linked to each other, in that a key click on a detail of one graphic (e.g., a specific product category on a sales pie chart) will immediately update the content of other graphics (e.g., the list of top product suppliers in another chart).

- *Any information, to anyone, anywhere*: Dashboards are highly customizable to display the information and analytics most important to particular users or communities. They can also be configured to deliver their content and alerts to almost any media or devices, locally or remotely networked.

Dashboards are *the* most popular portal from which most analytics and decision-making activities are launched and proceed. By seamlessly bringing together disparate information and business intelligence (BI) applications to a single focal point, they enable knowledge workers to accelerate the pace at which they can make intelligent decisions.

Mashups and Web 2.0

Mashups and related Web 2.0 technologies have more recently arrived on the scene to energize traditional dashboard solutions with both the interconnectivity and collaborative capabilities of popular social networking facilities and the individual empowerment of rapid development and deployment.

On the surface, mashup pages look very much like a typical dashboard, but it's what's under the covers that makes them special and highly suited to the New Intelligence world. Based on next-generation Web 2.0 technology, mashups support individually customized interfaces matched with an enhanced degree of information and user interconnectivity that take dashboards to the next level. Mashup pages are assembled by end users themselves from collections of data feeds and widgets that are developed, maintained, and customized by the greater community of users according to well-accepted standards and lightweight processes. In this environment, everyone has the potential to develop individually, or in collaboration with dozens (or hundreds) of peers, finely tailored dashboards uniquely adapted to the individual, without the requirement for deep software development skills or lengthy development cycles.

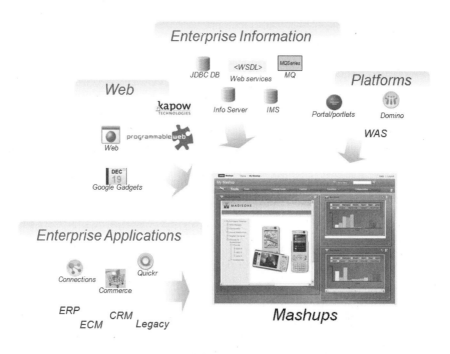

Figure 2.9: A variety of data sources feed mashups

As depicted in Figure 2.9, data feeds can be constructed or adapted to source any kind of data, information, or analytics, from anywhere, including internal and external sources. Examples include relational databases, OLAP cubes, web services applications, XML sources, spreadsheets, commercial news feeds, public services, and the like. Data feeds can be combined, transformed, or augmented as needed to synthesize the required information. In short, any information from anywhere. . . now that's interconnected! Likewise, graphical and textual widgets can be created or adapted using relatively simple tools to present the information in any desired format or interactive graphical visualization. As in the case of dashboards, mashup pages can be interactive, hot-linked, and context-sensitive. Unlike a typical dashboard, mashups provide end users with a practical means to rapidly create a visualization of the information they need, just for them. This yields an unprecedented opportunity for intelligence value to the individual, yet it's equally available to all in the organization.

As a descendent of the social networking phenomena, mashups lend themselves naturally to collaboration and human interconnectivity. Inherent to mashups are facilities for annotation and rating, as well as repositories and catalogs of existing information feeds and widgets. Mashups truly take dashboards to the next level, and directly address the New Intelligence challenges of variety and velocity.

Search

Expanding on the themes of variety and velocity—and now also adding volume—in this interconnected world of New Intelligence, advanced search technologies have opened new doors of opportunity to empower more users to make better decisions. Search has grown from its early days of specialty engines crawling the World Wide Web looking for and indexing pages into a highly diverse class of technologies that can be integrated or embedded in almost anything to search for almost anything in whatever context.

Still concerned with finding documents on a particular topic, search is now also about finding relevant information in the context of a business process for a given user. The sources and formats of this information have diversified to an enormous extent, beyond the well-structured tables, columns, and metrics that have been the domain of traditional analytics. Frequently cited research reveals that some 80% of new data content is unstructured; that is, it's contained in documents, e-mails, case notes, call logs, press articles, blogs, chat streams, images, videos, application logs, and unstructured records (e.g., XML) of every kind. This enormous body of content contains valuable and relevant information critical to intelligent decision-making, and it must be tapped. It must be combined with traditional structured metrics to rapidly build as complete a picture as possible upon which to base good conclusions.

Thus, search is now tightly integrated into the pervasive delivery of analytics content and applications, most notably in dashboards and mashups. Even as diverse information sources are consolidated and intelligently presented to a user on a single page, search provides the means to discover additional content on the fly. Clicking on a competitor's stock symbol might find the most recent new product announcements or acquisitions; drilling down into a troublesome inventory chart can initiate a search of shipping logs that reveal a pattern of damaged merchandise; a competitor's new product announcement might lead to a search of related technology patents. While dashboards and mashups already provide for linking content and applications, what distinguishes search is the unpredictable nature of the search request. Search allows the user to go where she needs to go, not where the application designer assumed she would go.

To better support New Intelligence, search is adaptive and extensible. It can learn from a user's pattern of behavior and navigation and tailor its results proactively. Thus, users can get more quickly to the most useful information that has the most value for them. The technology that enables such intelligent search is discussed in more detail in the following sections describing enterprise content and text analytics. Indeed, the growth of text analytics capabilities is the engine that drives the power of search within an analytics framework.

Analytic Infrastructure for New Intelligence

The delivery of analytics through the framework to the end user depends on a strong analytics infrastructure—the engines that access, transform, augment, consolidate, aggregate, and summarize data from any source into actionable information. This section reviews the analytic enablement processes, shown in Figure 2.10, available to support the analyst's daily activities.

Figure 2.10: Analytic process layer

Business Process Management

Business process management (BPM) is a discipline combining software capabilities and business expertise through people, systems, and information to accelerate time between process improvements, thus facilitating business innovation. Adding BI directly into the business process can improve the efficiency of human decision points. When a workflow gets routed to a decision-maker, it can be accompanied by timely and relevant information to support the process. By eliminating an ad hoc information-gathering step, decision makers can quickly act on items and render faster decisions.

Integrating BI into business processes also helps to improve the quality and consistency of decisions. By ensuring that uniform, up-to-date information is used for decision support, organizations can limit variability in human decisions—regardless of who is making those decisions. By directly integrating the information into the workflow, organizations can also ensure that information is always consulted prior to decision making. BPM extends beyond the software to include expertise and process assets, as shown in Figure 2.11.

BPM includes

Figure 2.11: BPM governs organizational and operational activities

To implement improved decision-making processes enriched by BI, organizations must carefully determine which information is most significant and relevant to any decision. Business analysts who are discovering and modeling processes must leverage enterprise-wide information to tie decision-related metrics to business outcomes. For example, when supporting a cross-sell/up-sell decision, analysts must look beyond immediate revenue goals to study lifetime customer value implications. Finding the right information can be a challenge, and organizations must foster collaboration between process owners and information management professionals to produce the best results. Information must also be included as part of the process improvement cycle. As processes are analyzed, improved, and redeployed, the value of decision-supporting information must continuously assessed and adjusted.

The ultimate way to boost the efficiency of business processes that contain complex decision points is to automate those decisions. Yet, given the complexity of many business decisions, automation is not always a viable option. However, by leveraging both process and BI metrics, organizations may be able to automate portions of these decisions.

Both process data and wider enterprise data are important to decision automation, as analysts must incorporate learning from previous decisions, as well as the implications for enterprise results. For example, process data may show that loan officers have approved loans 80% of the time when an applicant's credit score was higher than 600. Tying these approvals to enterprise results shows that 8% of these approved loans became delinquent, but that customers with other financial products from the bank were much less likely to default.

Key metrics from the business process and the BI system can be pieced together to drive rules and policies that automate portions of the workflow. Continuing the loan approval example, a business analyst may create a new business rule that automatically approves a loan application if the applicant's credit score is higher than 600 and they currently use one or more other services from the bank. Other applications would still be routed to loan officers for a decision.

Organizations can greatly improve the efficiency of processes when they automate even a portion of complex decision-making. By automating some operational decisions, workers can manage by exception, and focus on more critical and strategic activities. This process improvement is not always achievable, but by leveraging decision histories with enterprise information, it may be possible to find metrics that will drive the automation of workflows through decision points.

Business activity monitoring (BAM) is a critical component of BPM deployments and provides visibility into in-flight processes and enterprise applications. Without monitoring, automating business processes is risky and optimizing processes is impossible. A real-time view into process performance is essential for smooth operation, yet this view can be enhanced with additional information and insight provided by BI.

By linking BAM with BI, users can quickly investigate process metrics and analyze the broader implications of process performance. This analysis is extremely helpful when determining corrective actions. For example, a key performance indicator (KPI) displayed on a business dashboard may show that insurance claims processing volume is below service-level goals. To determine corrective action, an analyst can drill down in the process data to see processing time and processing volume by claim type. At the same time, additional enterprise data delivered through BI can show the impact of processing volume on customer satisfaction, and ultimately churn, thus predicting how process performance may impact financial results. This additional context allows business analysts to accurately weigh the costs and benefits of any response to the KPI alert. BI can also be useful in determining which KPIs are relevant to monitor. By linking process performance with enterprise outcomes, business analysts can see which KPIs have the most significant impact on results.

Organizations can leverage BI to augment and improve BPM efforts and business processes in many ways. There are, however, a number of ways that BPM and business processes can be extended to BI interfaces, and ultimately to BI users, to drive organizational responsiveness.

Transactional and historical data can be a valuable source of business insight, and BI can provide the capability to dive into and analyze this data. Often, analysts are able to uncover valuable details that will shape organizational priorities and policies moving forward. Usually, businesses need to take immediate action to capitalize on these insights, yet organizations generally do not have the necessary direct links between operations and analysis. Analysts typically communicate findings through ad hoc channels, and managers must then make decisions and implement actions based on incomplete information.

BPM can immediately provide value to BI users by simply extending process data to the BI system. The enterprise and transactional data traditionally analyzed using BI systems is essentially the result of business processes, and process data can provide important context to analysis of this data. For example, an analysis of enterprise data for a whole-saler may show that the metric of "days outstanding" has been increasing. This financial metric is the direct result of the wholesaler's order-to-cash processes. By tying the process data to the financial results, an analyst can drill into the process elements to see how they are affecting results.

The ultimate goal of BI implementations is to leverage insight to improve performance, yet these BI systems do not always have access to the key real-time process data that shows how this performance is driven. Using Smart Analytics, by extending BPM data to the BI system, organizations can make better strategic decisions supported by a complete, consistent view of the business.

IBM InfoSphere Streams

The goal of the IBM InfoSphere Streams is to provide breakthrough technologies that en-able aggressive production and management of information and knowledge from relevant data, which must be extracted from enormous volumes of potentially unimportant data. Specifically, the goal of InfoSphere Streams is to radically extend the state of the art in information processing by simultaneously addressing several technical challenges, including:

- Responding quickly to events and changing requirements

- Performing a continuous analysis of data at rates that are orders of magnitude greater than existing systems

- Adapting rapidly to changing data forms and types

- Managing high-availability, heterogeneity, and distribution for the new stream paradigm

- Providing security and information confidentiality for shared information

Stream computing is a new paradigm. In "traditional" processing, one can think of run-ning queries against relatively static data: for instance, "List all personnel residing within 50 miles of New Orleans." This query will result in a single result set. With stream com-puting, one can execute a process similar to a "continuous query," one that identifies per-sonnel who are currently within 50 miles of New Orleans, but can also get continuous, updated results as location information from GPS data is refreshed over time. In the first case, questions are asked of static data; in the second case, data is continuously evaluated by static questions. InfoSphere Streams goes further by allowing the continuous queries to be modified over time. A simple view of this distinction is shown in Figure 2.12.

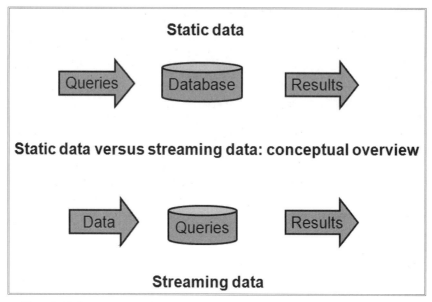

Figure 2.12: Streams processing versus traditional processing

Although other systems embrace the stream computing paradigm, InfoSphere Streams takes a fundamentally different approach to continuous processing and differentiates with its distributed runtime platform, programming model, and tools for developing continuous processing applications. The data streams consumable by InfoSphere Streams can originate from sensors, cameras, news feeds, stock tickers, or a variety of other sources, including traditional databases.

Emerging Use Cases

As InfoSphere Streams becomes a generally available offering, a number of applications are being pursued. The following provides a summary of the pilots conducted by IBM, highlighting the types of usage that can be supported by InfoSphere Streams.

- *Radio Astronomy*: A key strength of InfoSphere Streams lies in its ability to perform analytics on data-intensive streams to identify those few items that merit deeper investigation. One example of this use case is in the domain of radio astronomy. A number of projects globally receive continuous streams of telemetry from radio telescopes. For example, these radio telescopes might have thousands or tens of thousands of antennae, all routing data streams to a central supercomputer to survey a location in the universe. The InfoSphere Streams middleware running on that supercomputer can provide a more flexible approach to processing these streams of data. IBM is working with a university to develop analytics that identify anomalous and transient behavior such as high-energy cosmic ray bursts.

- *Energy Trading Services (ETS)*: The ETS pilot demonstrates how InfoSphere Streams can support energy trading. The demonstrated system provides energy traders with real-time analysis and correlation of events affecting energy markets, and allows them to make informed decisions faster than before. Analysis supporting energy traders include various heat maps, energy demand models, technical analysis of energy futures (Bollinger band, volume-weighted average price, etc.), news feed analysis to identify and evaluate energy-relevant events, and a map view of the predicted impact of a hurricane on the assets of oil companies. Traders can leverage shared computing infrastructure to obtain information quickly and at low cost. The system also provides context-sensitive guidance that helps traders select the best available sources and analytics for the task. The pilot uses Mashup Automation with Runtime Invocation and Orchestration (MARIO) to dynamically assemble applications needed by energy traders, deploying and operating the stream-processing parts of these applications in an InfoSphere Streams cluster. The set of 250 independent analytics, data sources, and configuration descriptions built for the ETS pilot are dynamically composed and parameterized in different combinations to create thousands of applications that analyze and present data relevant to energy trading.

- *Health monitoring*: Stream computing can be used to better perform medical analysis, with reduced workload on doctors. Privacy-protected streams of medical device data can be analyzed to detect early signs of disease, highlight correlations among multiple patients, and evaluate the efficacy of treatments. A strong emphasis is placed on data provenance in this domain, in tracking how data is derived as it flows through the system. A "First-of-its-Kind" collaboration between IBM and a U.S. university will use InfoSphere Streams to monitor premature babies in a neonatal unit.

Architectural Overview

The InfoSphere Streams architecture represents a significant change in computing system organization and capability. Even though it has some similarity to complex event processing (CEP) systems, it is built to support higher data rates and a broader spectrum of input data modalities. It also provides infrastructure support to address the needs for scalability and dynamic adaptability, like scheduling, load balancing, and high availability.

In InfoSphere Streams, continuous applications are composed of individual operators, which interconnect and operate on multiple data streams. Data streams can come from outside the system or be produced internally as part of an application. The following flow diagram (Fig. 2.13) shows how multiple sources of varying types of streaming data can be filtered, classified, transformed, correlated, and/or fused to inform equities trade decisions, using dynamic earnings calculations, adjusted according to earnings-related news analyses, and real-time risk assessments such as the impact of impending hurricane damage.

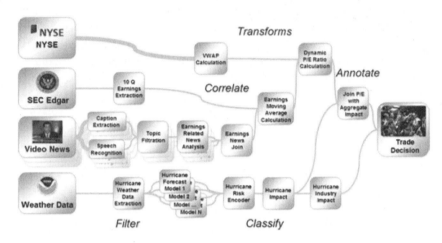

Figure 2.13: Trading example

For the purposes of this overview it is not necessary to understand the specifics of Figure 2.13; rather, its purpose is to demonstrate how streaming data sources from outside InfoSphere Streams can make their way into the core of the system, be analyzed in different fashions by different pieces of the application, flow through the system, and produce results. These results can be used in a variety of ways, including their display within a dashboard, their use to drive business actions, or their storage in enterprise databases for further offline analysis.

InfoSphere Streams can radically extend the state of the art in information processing by applying analytical processes to streaming and traditional data, thus providing organizations an incredible competitive advantage over their database-bound competition.

Online Analytical Processing (OLAP)

We have discussed MD analysis in its spreadsheet form and through graphical tooling such as Cognos. OLAP takes MD analysis to the next level of capability by allowing much higher data volumes, more complex analytics, and speed-of-thought response time. OLAP takes MD analysis out of front-end tooling and places it in the warehouse, where all users share one copy of the data and one copy of the analytical method. We have all experienced purchasing a car and financing that purchase, but have you noticed how your amortization calculator sometimes produces a different monthly payment than what the bank is charging you? This is because people tend to use algorithms they are accustomed to, and not all algorithms will produce the same result on a given set of data.

A single OLAP system can replace many thousands of spreadsheets, each sharing one copy of the data and one copy of the calculations. However, each time an OLAP system is built, we still face separate disconnected data marts and the complexities of managing them. Figure 2.14 could be expanded to show many OLAP cubes, a situation very often encountered, and easily circumvented, by imbedding OLAP capability within the warehouse as IBM has done with InfoSphere Warehouse.

Figure 2.14: Multidimensional spreadsheets in one OLAP cube

IBM's approach is to provide OLAP in the warehouse, so that no additional datamarts are required. This can produce:

- Cost savings in the form of:

  » Less hardware for data storage.

  » Lower licensing costs from less software on fewer machines.

  » Reduced costs of operations and maintenance for activities, such as software updates, backup/recovery, data capture and synchronization, data transformations, and problem resolution.

  » Reduced costs of resources required for support, including the cost of training and ongoing skills maintenance. This cost is particularly high in a heterogeneous environment.

- Reduced networking for connectivity and operations.

- Increased productivity: Data consolidation results in more productivity from an IT perspective, because the available resources have to be trained in fewer software products and hardware environments.

- Improved data quality and integrity: There is a significant advantage that can restore or even enhance user confidence in the data. Implementation of common and consistent data definitions, as well as managed update cycles, can result in query and reporting results that are consistent across the business functional areas of the enterprise.

This notion of a single data source for all analytics has been an elusive goal for businesses for some time now. With InfoSphere Warehouse, we are closer to that goal. A key methodology to enable this single data source is by *embedding analytics in the data warehouse.* InfoSphere Warehouse Cubing Services achieves this goal by leveraging the OLAP metadata stored in the data warehouse, which exposes a well-structured cubing environment to enhance users' analytic capabilities.

OLAP analytics, which has previously required data to be moved out of the data warehouse, results in the creation of multiple silos of information. Now OLAP analytics can be performed *without moving the data out of the data warehouse.* This *no-copy analytics* capability provides a significant advantage.

OLAP, using InfoSphere Warehouse Cubing Services, not only enables a single data source for analytics, but it also enables *near-real-time analytics* as a result of the reduced latency in getting access to the data.

IBM InfoSphere Entity Analytics Solutions

Good data practices in warehousing will result in a single version of the truth, be it customer name or product description. But where does the single version of the truth reside in the warehouse? Master Data Management (MDM) systems usually provide that single version of the truth, and the warehouse is thus a target for the MDM process. This really makes sense, as a great deal of effort and programming goes into building an MDM system, but how do we deal with incoming data when a person is trying to hide his identity, or when incomplete information is obtained? IBM provides InfoSphere Entity Analytics Solution to assist in verifying identity, even when the person is attempting to avoid detection. IBM InfoSphere Entity Analytic Solutions (EAS) dynamically manages the context, whereby each new transaction incrementally builds on what was known in real-time. Placing real-time transactions into context first enables new levels of BI.

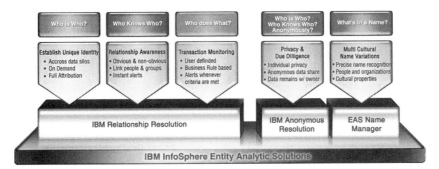

Figure 2.15: IBM InfoSphere Entity Analytic Solutions

Here, we will only look at the first two components of Figure 2.15: Identity Resolution (establish unique identity) and Relationship Resolution (relationship awareness).

Entity resolution is the process of identifying who is who (for people and organizations). For example, in criminal circles, it is accepted that individuals may possess multiple identities: the role of entity resolution is to establish all of the transactions that pertain to a single entity. For example, EAS helped one organization determine that they did not in fact have 120 distinct customer accounts; rather, all these accounts belonged to one person. Understanding who is who is fundamental to understanding context. One major challenge businesses face is that information about entities is invariably inconsistent. Is Bill really William? Are the month and day in the date of birth backward? Are the first and last names transposed? Is "S. Main Street" really supposed to be "South Maine Avenue?" Unlike the traditional management techniques that are common within data quality products, EAS recognizes that, when it comes to data about people and organizations, there is no single/best version of truth. Rather these natural variations are all potential valuable clues for future discovery.

Relationship resolution is the process whereby EAS establishes that there exists (or has existed) a relationship between different individuals. For example:

- Two people lived in the same house at the same time.

- A new employee's emergency contact information (in the payroll system) is one and the same as a recently arrested criminal.

- A large vendor has the same telephone number as an employee.

Admittedly, not every relationship matters. Just because two people live together, for example, two customers who are also roommates, does not warrant any additional attention. While EAS learns of such relationships and remembers these over time, only discoveries of relevance are issued as alerts (e.g., your purchasing manager lives with the vendor).

EAS understands expressed relationships (a reference on an employment application) and detects unexpressed relationships (roommates or people sharing an address or phone number). Understanding context in the form of who is related to who provides critical insight to maximize opportunities with customers, improve customer acquisition and retention, and mitigate risk.

How can EAS make your Smart Analytic system even better? EAS provides insight at the ingestion of data for real-time discovery. New observations are reconciled and related to historical data. Context and discovery accumulate incrementally in real time. Insight is pushed to users. Users do not have to pose smart questions to obtain valuable insights into identities and relationships. The system discovers relevance in real-time, within streams of data, and alerts users or systems of such insight.

Data Mining

Data mining technology has been actively evolving over the past few decades. The latest trend is to embed data mining in business processes and end-user applications within the New Intelligence workplace. The objective is to enable business-focused end users who are not experts in data mining but who do understand how to leverage data mining results to solve many common business problems.

Data mining uses advanced statistical techniques and mathematical algorithms to analyze usually very large volumes of historical data. The objectives of data mining are to discover and model unknown or poorly understood patterns and behaviors inherent in the data, thus creating descriptive and/or predictive models to gain valuable insights and predict outcomes with high business value. Such insights and the ability to predict responses can greatly enhance a decision-maker's ability to make smarter business decisions, leading to better service, lower costs, and higher profitability. Data mining has a wide variety of high-value business applications in many different industries and scenarios. The following examples illustrate just a few of the many scenarios in which data mining can demonstrably add significant value:

- *Cross-selling, upselling, promotion design, revenue acceleration, customer loyalty*: Discovering customer segments (illustrated in Figure 2.16) and the distinct purchasing patterns, item affinities, and most likely next purchases within each segment

- *Customer retention*: Predicting which high-value customers are at risk of churning

- *Disease management*: Predicting which patients are at high risk of being hospitalized or developing a certain disease; disease progression; drug interactions; cohort selection; treatment outcomes

- *Quality assurance, warranty claims mitigation*: Predicting which parts are likely to fail together or sequentially; discovering root causes of part failures or production problems

- *Fraud detection*: Discovering high-potential groups of claims or individuals

- *Category management, inventory management*: Predicting out-of-stocks or overstocks; replenishment of related items in anticipation of increased promotional sales of a given item; store/branch profiling

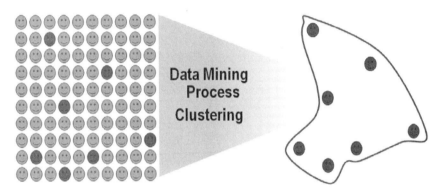

Figure 2.16: Data mining clustering example: discovering customers with similar buying behavior

Data mining includes both descriptive and predictive techniques. Descriptive mining methods (sometimes called "unsupervised learning") include clustering (segmentation), associations (link analysis), and sequences (temporal links). One example is customer segmentation to discover one or more high-potential segments of customers to target in a promotional campaign, combined with associations and/or sequences to help design the promotion (promoted item and affinity items) and to guide stocking decisions in anticipation of increased sales. Predictive mining methods (sometimes called "supervised learning") include classification and regression. An example is loan default prediction using a decision tree classification model to predict which customers are at high risk of defaulting on their loans and to determine what the major predictors of default are.

Once a data mining model has been trained (built and validated) using historical data, it can be applied to new or existing records (customers, claims, etc.) to predict outcomes, assign individuals to their respective best-fit segments, or find the highest-likelihood next decision or event for a given individual in a process called *scoring*. Scoring processes may be implemented in batch mode (e.g., scheduled rescoring of loan customers to update each one's default risk for a weekly report) or in real-time mode (e.g., scoring a customer during the course of an online or call-center transaction for loan approval or a cross-sell offer). Scoring may be accomplished through an end-user application (e.g., portal application for a call center representative) or an automated process (e.g., website application capable of automatically scoring and making real-time offers for affinity items when a customer adds a given item to his shopping cart; automated update of a customer's propensity to purchase a life insurance policy when a certain life change occurs, triggering a mailing with an offer).

While some data mining models may be fine-tuned for a specialized problem type in a specific domain, the mining solution approaches to many business problems can be generalized from one domain to another. For example, the customer churn problem in telco is conceptually similar to the risk of disease in healthcare. Industry-specific parameters may vary, but the fundamental concept of predicting a certain outcome is the same.

Data mining can be performed and utilized in different ways by a spectrum of users throughout an enterprise, depending on the business objectives and operational organization. First, using either a data mining workbench tool, in-database mining capabilities, or a combination thereof, a data mining expert may create mining models for ad hoc purposes to address certain (often complex) problems. Such a model may serve a one-time purpose without being deployed to a wider group of users or analysts.

Second, a data mining expert may create mining models that are implemented through end-user applications, in which the mining results are incorporated into reports or interactive applications for customer-facing employees or executives.

Third, data mining capabilities may be embedded in user applications through which business analysts can execute "guided" data mining and consume the mining results as part of analytic reports, (e.g., a retail store clustering application used by category managers).

Fourth, data mining modeling and scoring may be incorporated into automated operational processes, such as an automated modeling process to refresh (update) a data mining model as new data becomes available. For example, real-time updated data can be used in an application that predicts the propensity to purchase items online during the Olympics as favorites emerge during a popular event; used in an automated scoring process to trigger an action when records are updated, such as notifying an insurance agent to contact his customer with a life insurance upsell offer when a new dependent is added; or used to alert sales when certain types of transactions occur, such as issuing a real-time cross-sell offer to an online shopper.

One of the great advantages of in-database mining, compared to mining in a separate analytical environment, is direct access to the data in its primary store rather than having to move data back and forth between the database and the analytical environment. In a data warehousing environment, data mining operates over the data *in* the database, without expensive and time-consuming extracts to external structures. This approach enables the mining functions to operate with lower latency, supporting real-time or near-real-time mining as data arrives in the data warehouse, particularly with automated mining processes.

Time-series analysis techniques can predict a data series into the future, such as monthly sales forecast for the coming year. Unlike many data mining techniques that work best with large amounts of data and that find patterns and relationships among many data fields, time-series analysis can generate forecasts of individual fields with comparatively small ("spreadsheet-sized") data sets.

To drive effective and intelligent decisions, data mining must be integrated into the analytics framework and provide consumable interaction with end users. Implementation of mining results includes the development and deployment of end-user interfaces to invoke mining functions and deliver results in the form of visualizations or tables that can be readily incorporated into the reporting, analytics, dashboards, and mashups comprising the top of the analytics framework hierarchy. Design tooling needs to provide easy-to-use graphical editors and wizards to simplify data preparation and modeling tasks. Once deployed, users need easy interfaces to invoke the mining methods, through industry standards such as Structured Query Language (SQL), Open Database Connectivity (ODBC), Java, and Web Services. They should seamlessly integrate into existing application and Service Oriented Architecture (SOA) configurations. They must provide interactive visualizations or deliver results in other appropriate forms to make mining discoveries and insights understandable, consumable, and ultimately actionable.

Data mining can provide value to other processes using industry-standard Predictive Model Markup Language (PMML). PMML enables the exchange of data mining models across common business applications or systems, thus allowing models from different sources to be incorporated into business processes. For example, a model created within SPSS and exported in PMML format can be imported into a DB2 database and integrated into an in-database scoring process, thus leveraging the power of a large warehousing environment.

Text Analytics

Closely related to, and in some ways growing out of advances in data mining and search, is the emerging field of text analytics. Traditional data mining operates best on tightly organized structured and numeric data. But we've already revealed that 80% of the new data and the vast majority of information useful to decision making is neither structured nor tightly organized. It is free text contained in a plethora of formats (XML, CSV, text, spreadsheets, source documents and presentations, PDFs, etc.). The wealth of information in unstructured content cannot be ignored, and it must be discovered, analyzed, mined, and revealed. Text analytics provides technologies and methods to do just that.

Text analytics seeks to find the useful information, key phrases, and metrics held within a sometimes vast collection of free text. At the end of the day, analytics and reporting needs structure and context: We can't compare or add two numbers if we don't have the structure and context around those numbers, such as the sales values for shoes for the past two quarters. It is not practical to consider exhaustive structuring of text data when 80% of our information is free-form. To illustrate, consider the cost in time and system resources required to "shred" every XML document (which are at least semi-structured) into a form suitable for structured (relational) storage and access. Now consider the cost of doing this to all free text content in the organization. The costs and information duplication would be astronomical. Therefore, text analytics examines free text within the context of a particular domain (e.g., retail, crime investigation, or vegetable farming) and annotates the free text with structured metadata. These annotations provide the "structured" content needed for fruitful reporting, analytics, and BI.

The most effective text analytics method to emerge in the information industry is based on the Unstructured Information Management Architecture (UIMA) standards. Evolved from joint industry and academic research (of which IBM has been a major contributor, and the first vendor to go to market with commercial UIMA-based offerings), UIMA provides an extensible framework for text analytics. This adaptability is critical to its role in the New Intelligence world.

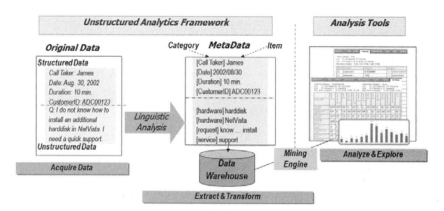

Figure 2.17: Text analytics flow of information

As shown in Figure 2.17, text analysis within a UIMA framework has three stages:

1. Data ingestion

2. Natural-language processing and indexing (annotating)

3. Visualization and interactive mining

Data ingestion involves accessing the data in a common form, usually XML, regardless of the original source.

The next phase, *natural-language processing*, is the heart of UIMA-based text analytics, the phase in which discovery and analysis takes place. This includes a series of several customizable processes, including:

- *Concept extraction*: Key concept words (domain specific) are noted in the source text and matched to a broader range of synonyms and related concepts. Semantic dictionaries (customizable) and pattern matching rules are used to identify context-specific words and phrases.

- *Intention analysis*: Uses the semantic dictionary and pattern matching to classify common grammatical expressions. For example, verbs followed by "cannot," "can't," or "failed" might be classified as "problems." Problems can then be further grouped and analyzed. Phrase subjects are matched to problem phrases to identify a meaningful concept: "The brakes are broken."

- *Extensible and customizable editors*: Dictionary and rules editors allow organizations to obtain freely or commercially available components and extend or modify them to meet their specific business requirements, such as a customer support call center, a fraud detection department, or a study of medical records.

Visualization and mining of the results is supported through high-performance index structures and interactive text mining components. The visualization process provides a graphical view of annotation results: concept frequencies and distribution, time series distributions, trends, trend anomalies, and concept correlations.

Annotated results are the high-value outputs of UIMA-based text analysis. These metadata tags provide structure and metrics to previously unstructured data. This allows information gleaned from unstructured sources to now be aggregated and correlated with traditional structured data, for example to perform typical OLAP analysis of a sales cube, combined with customer support feedback in free text. These new tags also enable a much higher level of advanced search. Previously undetected free-text concepts may now be indexed and searched, providing heretofore unattainable search accuracy and value.

Text analytics is a backbone technology to support the new business challenges surrounding information variety, volume, and velocity.

Content Management

Enterprise content management (ECM) covers a wide array of technologies and processes focused on managing all the variety and volumes of information collected and maintained by an organization. More than just maintaining repositories of documents, it is focused on transforming those assets into valuable information that can be used in intelligent business processes and decisions. All forms of content, the vast majority of which (some 80%) is unstructured, can be managed, including all business documents, web content, e-mail repositories, chat streams, video streams, images and graphics, electronic records, publications, reports, and more. Any report produced by the analytics framework can be managed by ECM.

It is not enough to simply archive this wealth of assets into a repository silo; effective ECM must make the information available to every business user and business process that needs it to influence and support intelligent business decisions and responses to dynamic events. ECM adds value to these assets by indexing, analyzing, and annotating (using text analytics and data mining); categorizing (using asset taxonomies); and then correlating information. These improved assets are then made available to those users and business processes that need them through open industry standard interfaces and programmatic application interfaces (APIs), so that they can optimize business performance management (BPM) and play a strong role in the analytics framework. High-value ECM assets can be integrated through direct linkage and powerful search to business analytics delivered in dashboards, mashups, and other applications. Through linkage with BPM and business process rules engines, these assets can be leveraged in support of policy compliance. They can be integrated through Web 2.0 and collaboration technologies to support the necessary information sharing among colleagues that drives better decision-making.

Figure 2.18 summarizes the major components of effective ECM. These are examined in more detail in the context of how better decisions are made more rapidly leveraging ECM in the analytics framework.

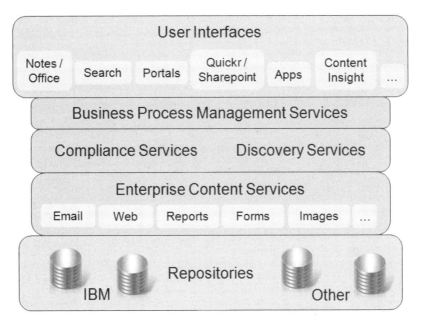

Figure 2.18: Key components of enterprise content management

- *The right information from anywhere*: Good decisions are made based on the best information, regardless of the source or content. Effective ECM manages and consolidates information from a variety of source repositories through its Enterprise Content Services facilities. These include facilities to access web content, e-mail, forms and records, reports, digital images and video, and more. Facilities for searching and securely delivering these assets are provided.

- *Deliver content intelligence—the right information*: Discovery and analytics services are provided to analyze, annotate, and categorize information assets. Using the features of data mining and text analytics described earlier, valuable business concepts and metrics are gleaned from the managed content, regardless of form or source, and are annotated to the assets. This intelligent metadata is leveraged by downstream analytics processes, BPM processes, and advanced search capabilities to support better decision-making. These services also ensure that the right information is delivered by matching key business concepts embedded in the information to the business process or individual request.

- *Enforce policies and compliance*: Compliance services are provided in the ECM solution to ensure that information assets are utilized correctly and securely, adhering to regulations and policies around privacy, government regulations, corporate governance, and the like. These services provide facilities for governing and maintaining the full lifecycle of the organization's information assets.

- *Deliver within the context of a business process, according to business rules*: The Business Process Management Services provides facilities to integrate and incorporate the enhanced and compliant information assets into day-to-day business processes and decisions, thus improving results and efficiencies. For example, these services enable a user handling an insurance claim to quickly access all relevant policy rules, case notes, and previous customer communications that contribute to a high-quality decision.

- *Enable pervasive and collaborative delivery of the information*: To provide maximum value, the information assets must be delivered to all users who need them, when they need them, and in the context they need them. This is accomplished through a collection of special-purpose tools and interfaces that enable popular industry-standard desktop tools such as Microsoft Excel and web browsers. Common interfaces, such as web services and Java APIs, can be leveraged to integrate content management assets into analytics applications, portals, dashboards, mashups, and more. Links to collaborative environments like Lotus Quickr and Microsoft Sharepoint enable effective sharing of information within a team for better decisions and outcomes.

The capabilities of ECM continue to expand, enabling organizations to discover and access more and more value within their rapidly growing wealth of unstructured content. Far beyond simply maintaining and archiving these information assets, ECM actively enables these assets to integrate with and play a leading role in the analytics framework, thus optimizing business processes and supporting more intelligent decision-making.

The Infrastructure Layer

Now that we have examined the user interface and the analytic process layers, let's look at those components that hold the system together: the infrastructure layer, as shown in Figure 2.19.

Figure 2.19: The infrastructure layer

IBM InfoSphere Warehouse

IBM InfoSphere Warehouse can help companies extract insight from virtually any type of data—helping to deliver the right information at the right time, so that business leaders can make the right decisions. The InfoSphere Warehouse solution integrates data warehousing and business analytics to help define a company's central business concepts and the data required to support those concepts from an enterprise-wide perspective. It allows organizations to pull data from source systems that traditional BI and data warehousing solutions cannot access, which makes it easier for IT organizations to support business requirements for actionable information—not just raw data, but data with intelligence behind it to help people take action and make sound business decisions.

IBM InfoSphere Warehouse is a complete, multipurpose environment that allows companies to access, analyze, and act on operational and historical information—whether structured or unstructured—thus enabling them to get the insight and agility they need to consistently generate new opportunities, contain costs, and satisfy customers. It is designed to be the first comprehensive data server that enables businesses to centrally, accurately, and securely analyze and deliver information as part of operational and strategic business applications. Unlike traditional data warehouses and BI approaches that are complex, nonintegrated, and rigid, InfoSphere Warehouse solutions simplify the processes of selecting, deploying, and maintaining an affordable information management infrastructure that delivers the flexibility required by organizations to dynamically integrate and transform data into actionable business insight.

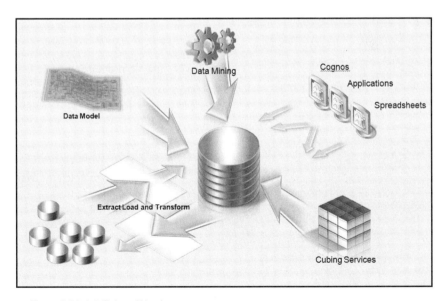

Figure 2.20: InfoSphere Warehouse

InfoSphere Warehouse has all the components to build a Smart Analytic system: DB2 database, physical data modeling, rich intra-DB2 transformations (ETL), SQL-based ETL, data mining, text analytics, and OLAP. These functions (Fig. 2.20) are integrated through metadata sharing and a common set of tooling to increase the developer's productivity and decrease application deployment time.

IBM Smart Analytics System

As discussed throughout this book, today's business world demands rapid adaptability and response to frequently changing business conditions, challenges, and opportunities, while simultaneously demanding vigilant attention to cost efficiency and resource conservation. InfoSphere Warehouse has shown the value of an inclusive analytics warehouse platform for delivering intelligent BI solutions. The next step is to take this software platform and extend it to deliver a more complete solution for New Intelligence, out of the box.

While the pace of business continues to increase, the time and effort required to assemble from scratch the components of a smart solution based on the analytics framework is daunting indeed. Organizations need services and offerings that can jump-start the process of deploying an effective solution while at the same time retaining all of the high-value services and features that intelligent business requires. The new IBM Smart Analytics System provides just that acceleration to a solution that modern business is looking for.

Analytics Software

➤ Business Intelligence Solution

➤ Embedded analytics framework

Data Warehouse Platform

➤ Database server

➤ Scalability, optimization, workload management, high availability

System Platform

➤ Hardware, CPU, Storage

➤ Operating System

Figure 2.21: IBM Smart Analytics System stack

The IBM Smart Analytics System stack (Fig. 2.21) is an integrated high-performance analytics system for accelerating delivery of insights for faster and smarter action. Designed for modular scalability, it is able to adjust and grow based on changing business requirements, providing:

- Broad analytics capabilities

- A robust data warehouse platform

- Fully integrated and scalable IBM hardware systems

- A single point of support for the system, not disparate component parts

This new system is preconfigured and preoptimized for rapid deployment for any size of solution, delivering results in a matter of days instead of the months required for alternative piece-part approaches. The primary value of this solution is its ability to deliver powerful analytics how, where, and when needed: a key requirement for New Intelligence. The integrated analytics features of the IBM Smart Analytics System map closely to the hierarchical analytics framework described in this chapter.

Advanced reporting, scorecards, dashboards, and analytic applications are provided to deliver analytics to the end users in the form and context required for the business process at hand. Based on the powerful Cognos Business Intelligence software platform, these services enable businesses to:

- Uncover new opportunities, for example, through data discovery, mining, and OLAP analysis

- Obtain fast answers to business questions, as through advanced dashboard and reporting technology built on a platform to fully leverage the underlying analytics framework

- Make better decisions faster through high-performance integration with analytics services, including text analytics and search

- Optimize business performance using Cognos' powerful BI platform and best practices

The Business Intelligence layer (based on Cognos software, described in Chapter 3) is built on and integrated with the analytics framework infrastructure, providing deep business analysis with multidimensional (OLAP) services, embedded data mining, and unstructured text analytics. These capabilities are integrated directly into the IBM Smart Analytics System platform and the data warehouse layer to provide high-performance analytics directly on the warehouse data without wasteful duplication and lengthy outboard computations. The analytics is built-in directly to the system and pushed seamless out to the users through the Cognos Business Intelligence layer.

All of this powerful analytics runs atop an enterprise-class DB2 warehouse providing highly scalable and reliable access to data and information. Advanced workload management features in the data warehouse are preconfigured to accelerate and optimize the analytics capabilities.

The software platform is delivered on a robust and scalable IBM hardware foundation built on Power technology and AIX. The entire system, hardware and software, is entirely modular, allowing businesses to add new modules as requirements change, with increasing numbers of users, increasing data volumes, new functional or analytical requirements, or any combination of these. Because all modules are preconfigured and optimized, they can be rapidly deployed to address new demands. With its fully integrated architecture, the IBM Smart Analytics System delivers the analytics framework in a complete solution package, thus lowering implementation and deployment costs while accelerating the time to value and results.

IBM Smart Analytics Optimizer

While the IBM Smart Analytics System offers a revolutionary end-to-end hardware/software stack for powerful BI solutions, the IBM Smart Analytics Optimizer adds another new module to that architecture, one specifically designed to dramatically speed analytics. Combining hardware and software technology, the IBM Smart Analytics Optimizer can offload significant query workload from the database server to a separate processor, improving both the query performance of the offloaded queries, but also improving overall query performance for the workload that remains on the data server.

The IBM Smart Analytics Optimizer utilizes powerful new in-memory database technology and routes queries that would have gone to the data server to its own processor. This routing and optimization is completely transparent to the tools and applications that issue the queries, but the performance gains will not be transparent to those end users and business processes that benefit from them. Reporting and other analytical applications will realize a significant performance boost, many by an order of magnitude. Thus, the addition of this kind of optimization technology only serves to increase the rate of response to business questions and increasing business analytics demands.

Getting Our Minds Around the New Intelligence

This chapter has reviewed the activities of business analysts and the tools they use to make their decisions, the data warehouse processes that support these tools, and the infrastructure that holds the whole process together. Smart Analytics is not just a new warehouse and a new set of user tools, but a collaborative and responsive system, capable of taking your business into the new realm of business in a Smart Planet.

3

New Intelligence
Business Intelligence and
Performance Management

So far, we have discussed the various analytic functions and types that most organizations use or evaluating to enhance the data provided to their users. Data warehouses and infrastructure technologies are essential elements for the preparation, building, and maintenance of the underpinning data and infrastructure. The components that provide the visible value to the infrastructure are Business Intelligence (BI) and Performance Management (PM) tools.

Businesses today must be able to answer a broad range of questions in far less time than in the past. Information can no longer be cloistered in silos, nor can it be looked at as being the purview of a selected group. To maximize the business value of an organization's data, it is essential to have an Information Agenda. Such an agenda entails being able to access and deliver any and all information to the correct individuals in the context of their business requirements. It must be agile, flexible, and eliminate delays that could affect the decision-making process.

BI and PM solutions have been used for years to provide additional insight and analysis on key information. However, these solutions have taken on exponential importance in recent years and are considered mission-critical by many organizations. In this chapter, we describe and discuss how to be more effective and visionary in the usage and application of these tools and technologies, with a focus on IBM's Cognos 8 suite.

Business Issues

- Too much information and not knowing what's important
  - Not using demand signals to drive supply chain
  - Not using customer analysis to tailor marketing and sales
  - Not leveraging valuable unstructured information
- Multiple versions of the truth
  - Problems managing customer, product and partner interactions
  - Regulatory compliance inhibited by poor transparency
- Lack of trusted information
  - Incomplete, out-of-date, inaccurate, misinterpreted data
  - Difficult to understand or control how information is used
- Lack of agility
  - Inability to take advantage of opportunities for innovation
  - Escalating costs due to inflexible systems and changing needs

Figure 3.1: Customer business issues

As shown in Figure 3.1, customers have articulated a set of common concerns. Many of these problem areas surface when either when applying BI/PM technologies or when acquiring the tools to address them. Given that many industry pundits predict a massive uptake in BI solutions by 2012, in order for this growth to occur, several fundamental changes must take place within the typical organization.

Here, we will address each of the problem areas listed in Figure 3.1 within the context of BI and PM solutions. Three of them are usually brought to attention after the delivery of inaccurate or out-of-date information. We often hear the lament, "We have multiple versions of the truth." Obviously, this is irrational because there can only be one truth regarding information; what people are really saying is that they have a huge volume of data and yet can't find what they need or can't deliver information in a timely manner.

Typically, the root of the problem is the lack of a fully integrated data infrastructure. When, for example, a sale is made of some widget to Mr. John Doe of 123 Main Street, Cincinnati, OH 45202, and he pays $34.90 + tax on 2/14/09, the information about this transaction may take a convoluted journey through the seller's enterprise data domain, where it will be used in a multitude of ways.

At the granular layer, when a customer service representative takes a call from Mr. Doe or we wish to promote some new product to our customers, we need to know how much business Mr. Doe does with us. In this context, we need very up-to-date and accurate information. Our company's widget buyer must have an accurate inventory of widgets, but her need for up-to-date information will depend upon the internal buying cycle. In the accounting department, the need is for accurate sales and tax information pertinent to Mr. Doe's purchase.

But what if what really happened was that Mr. Doe bought not a widget, but another object that had been mislabeled, and neither he nor the clerk paid any attention to the details of the sale? And what if John didn't like the thing after he tried it and returned it for credit later? This one transaction with its little foibles and miscues is just another piece of data generated in the course of doing business. What is relevant here is the need to capture, rollup, and reflect all aspects of such information as rapidly as possible. Insulating end users from errors and applying changes as rapidly as possible can only be accomplished when one enables a dynamic data infrastructure that is totally accurate and extremely agile.

The ability to easily plug BI/PM elements into a corporate Service Oriented Architecture (SOA) platform is key to attaining this growth. Note also that the reference is to a BI *platform*: The implication here is that there exists a comprehensive suite of BI functionality available for imbedding and delivering a wide range of functions.

Gain Insight from the Information Explosion
Smarter integrated solutions help you manage, protect, process, and analyze unprecedented volumes of structured and unstructured data—creating insight that drives innovation and business optimization

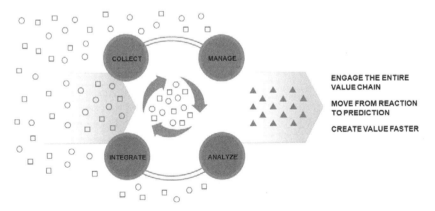

Figure 3.2: Getting smart about the information explosion

So, you've been hearing a lot about "smart" in this book (Fig. 3.2). How do BI and PM solutions help you operate and act smarter? Numerous surveys have been taken about the use and effectiveness of BI and PM solutions, and here's what they've shown:

1. Business intelligence and performance management has emerged as the top investment priority for CIOs.

2. The uptake by the user population is still low compared to the overall potential population in the enterprise.

3. One of the key factors in BI success, a Competency Center, is often lacking, thus limiting success.

4. Many organizations surveyed understand that they are losing revenue due to the inability to extract meaningful, relevant, current data.

One of the factors contributing to reduced success is that many an enterprise simply fails to select the proper BI/PM tools to make a difference. Many believe that BI should be easy, that all one needs to do is select a tool and gain access to the data. Later, we'll discuss BI tool selection in detail, but here suffice it to say that clearly defined goals, support, and a clear corporate mission must be in place if a business is to succeed in the effective deployment of BI/PM technologies.

Many organizations have invested heavily in data, data warehousing, analytics, infrastructure, and numerous tools, trying to provide themselves with a competitive edge and distance themselves from the competition. Some may have been more adept at creating these solutions than others.

Implementation of effective BI/PM solutions does not guarantee success. However, ineffective use of such technologies or improper and dated access to information does guarantee mediocrity. BI/PM solutions can provide information to drive intelligent decisions at all levels within the enterprise, and the success garnered by these actions is quantifiable and contagious, but numerous elements influence the effective application of BI and PM technologies.

Beginning with the data layer, some technologies provide data that is fresher, better organized, and easier to consume. In today's global environment, new, fresh data is generated continuously. If you are more effective at consuming information in a timely manner and distributing it rapidly within your BI infrastructure, it could provide a significant competitive edge. But BI/PM isn't just about data.

Some very critical factors affect success with BI/PM solutions. The top critical factors, borne out by years of implementing BI/PM solutions, include:

- *Data must have an Information Agenda*: The data must be accurate, timely, and relevant to provide input to key business analysis processes. An end-to-end data architecture must be in place that can address data flow in the ways that the enterprise requires it to be maximally effective.

- *Infrastructure must create a total solution stack*: The infrastructure (ETL, data warehouse, data access, and security) must be flexible, dynamic, and available, as well as secure. The continued support and promotion of individual silos of data and applications should be terminated.

- *BI/PM technologies selected must support the underlying infrastructure*: Such tools must be able to create and convey information that can be understood and acted upon by many individuals from many areas within the organization. These tools should support the entire data infrastructure. A process that is counter to the corporate data and infrastructure agendas should be promptly terminated. An example of this would be having to extract data after it is stored in the data warehouse, in order that a particular tool can use it more effectively.

- *Corporate vision and execution must have a plan and convey it to the enterprise*: Understand the value of BI/PM to the enterprise and convey this vision to all employees expected to utilize it. This critical issue is beyond the scope of this chapter, and is one that relies upon internal policies and politics, but we strongly suggest this is essential to any enterprise.

Now we'll look at how the IBM Cognos portfolio can deliver key business value to users throughout the enterprise. We will discuss the Cognos suite at a high level, as well as spend some time describing how best to drive value from BI and PM solutions. Despite the fact that all BI solutions may be similar in function (query, reporting, etc.), the proper selection of a BI/PM technology will make all the difference in delivering effective solutions that can change one's business.

IBM has launched the New Intelligence initiative with BI/PM as its key components. It is all about making smarter decisions in a shorter timeframe. Customers tell us that they know they need more information in a timely manner. They seem to sense that more effective use of BI/PM technologies can dramatically deliver incremental value in a more dynamic way. The question is, how do you do this? Do you just try harder, or are there things you need to change to be more effective? To begin, ask yourself if the systems and processes you have in place today deliver answers to three of the most commonly posed questions in any organization.

Three Critical Business Performance Questions

As we see in Figure 3.3, a modern BI/PM solution answers three common business questions that are essential to understanding a business and that drive better peformance:

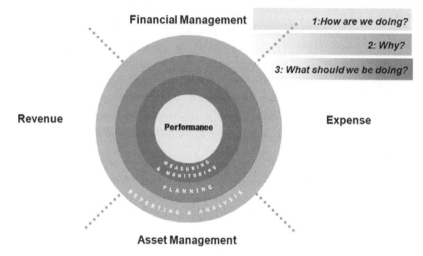

Figure 3.3: The three fundamental questions

1. How are we doing? Display where we are using dashboards and scorecards to give us a sense of our current status.

2. Why are we doing it (whatever it is)? Use reporting and analysis to quantify and hopefully qualify key metrics, trends, positions.

3. What should we be doing? Whether we are up or down, let's plan, budget, forecast, and run what-if scenarios . . . there are always areas where we can improve. Give us a view into the future.

Throughout the organization, decision-makers who contribute to corporate performance need the capabilities to find answers to these three basic questions. They need to be able to *measure and monitor* their business and share current status. That allows them to find answers to the question, "How are we doing?" To be able to dig down and determine why the situation is what it is, they need the capabilities of *reporting and analyzing to make sense of what has happened*. That gives them the ability to look at historic data and understand trends, to look at anomalies, to understand "why?"

Planning is the lynchpin between the two. Planning takes the understanding of what's going on and sets it into a forward-looking view of the business, which you measure and monitor against actual performance. Planning answers the question: *What should we be doing?* These integrated capabilities allow you to find answers to the fundamental questions that drive performance.

These answers enable you to respond to changes happening in your business and to make decisions that effectively drive your organization's performance. Every decision-maker is thinking about finding answers to these questions everyday. It's a fundamental cycle of business thinking. Not having the answers to any one of these questions leaves a gap that could cost your organization money.

An example of this flow of decision-making might be a quarterly report that shows revenues down 20% from last year. What do you do about it? A sales executive will ask for reports that answer several sales-related questions: Why did we miss our number? Did one region fall down? Are there some common competitive losses? Did the marketing campaign miss the mark? Once armed with the reports and analyses that answer these initial questions, he can adjust his sales plan going forward, continually monitoring progress against that plan. This is an iterative cycle that naturally flows from one question to the other.

BI/PM Tools Selection: Setting the Standard for the Enterprise

Previous generations of BI tools and technologies often led to the end-user mantra of, "If I could just get to my data!" The implication was that if users were provided access to the data across systems, silos, applications, formats, and platforms, all they would need was a BI tool that would let them do all the analysis themselves. In response, many tools were introduced that allowed access and analysis of data in a variety of ways. The Holy Grail then was to provide enough function for users to simply differentiate one tool from its competitors.

Both IT and end users quickly found that too many obstacles stood in the way of delivering a consistent, timely, single version of the truth, and this revelation paved the way for more orderly and BI-oriented architectures, such as data warehouses and data marts. However, silos of information were limited in their value across the enterprise, and the use of multiple tools in multiple areas proved costly and only partially effective.

Just about the time modern data warehousing and BI solutions were gaining ground on delivering effective and timely information within an enterprise, we saw the emergence of the Internet, along with a shift in the volume of data and its sources, and an entirely new set of end users. New standards such as XML emerged, accompanied by exponential increases in available information. The pressure never relents; the problems do not become smaller.

Significant challenges face any vendor wishing to provide a suite of tools that deliver the breadth and depth of function required in today's market. In the case of IBM Cognos, there are several basic tenets adhered to that keep it at the top of the BI spectrum:

- *Open standards*: The architecture must provide its rich set of functions using technologies and interfaces that are open and accepted in the industry. Closed, proprietary solutions are not appealing in today's market.

- *Interoperation with IBM technologies*: The IBM Cognos portfolio must be absorbed into IBM's massive technology stack and take advantage of its many complementary offerings (databases, metadata servers, Master Data Management, portals, and more).

- *Broad support for other vendor solutions*: IBM Cognos cannot exist in a vacuum. It must effectively support other databases, portals, Enterprise Resource Planning (ERP) solutions, and more.

The interoperability of components within an infrastructure is essential to delivering a comprehensive solution. If the individual components of a BI solution operate as separate pillars of function, there is little difference between a solution suite and a gaggle of independent BI tools. Given the many mergers and acquisitions in the BI space within the last few years, many providers are faced with how to best integrate a disparate set of tools into a cohesive offering.

IBM Cognos 8: A New Suite for a Smarter Planet

IBM Cognos 8 platform is a suite of BI and PM functions being fed by a metadata layer that provides consistency of data across the enterprise (Fig. 3.4). It is available on a wide variety of platforms from Windows to System z. It is fully integrated, such that a user or part of an organization may begin at any key functional area (query, reporting, online analytical processing [OLAP], financial performance, etc.) and work within a framework of a common set of functions with a single view of the data. This is the basis for delivering BI and PM with trusted information.

Now that we've seen the advantages and strengths of IBM's data warehouse technologies and infrastructure, let's make a basic set of assumptions as we enter into a deeper discussion of the IBM Cognos portfolio:

1. IBM's data warehouse portfolio addresses the requisite infrastructure onto which we can snap our BI and PM layer.

2. The concept of having a Smarter Planet driving New Intelligence is based upon access to all key information at the correct time, at the correct level for the end user, and in the context of the business problem at hand.

3. The metadata layer being provided to end users and applications operates seamlessly with the BI and PM applications, thus keeping the common view accurate and in sync.

Built on an SOA to deploy successfully within changing environments

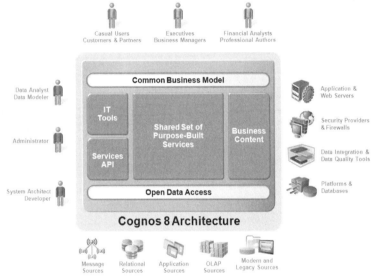

Figure 3.4: The IBM Cognos 8 architecture, a BI/PM platform for the intelligent enterprise

Let's begin with the bottom layer and work our way up through in the IBM Cognos 8 architecture.

Open Data Access

Any and all data held within the enterprise must be available for access by the BI/PM platform. Cognos 8 provides a path to a huge variety of data in all platforms, formats, and types. Special formats such as OLAP cubes must be available, as well as unstructured and semi-structured sources. Modern as well as legacy data must all be a part of the BI/PM infrastructure or its value to the enterprise is restricted.

Common Metadata Layer

Data definitions, as well as remapping of data, must be available to the right users within the context of their roles and functions. Without a common basis for the information that is accessed, BI/PM results are suspect. The Cognos metadata layer is highly customizable for use by all elements of the organization. Data may be defined in user terms, and access can be restricted to any or all individuals. The metadata layer is the window into the corporate data Information Agenda. It is that "single version of the truth" so often discussed but seldom delivered.

Data, once defined and validated, is presented to end users in *packages*. These are logical collections of the underpinning real data. Users may be assigned to one or more packages as required. Different packages for the same data may be meted out to adjust to differences in business terminology. Commonly used calculations may be defined in the metadata layer, thus providing a consistent version of a calculation rather than requiring every end user to create his own.

The lineage of the data from source to presentation is available to end users, so that they have no doubts concerning its origin, validity, and usage. Integration with IBM's Business Glossary adds depth to understanding what a particular data element means within the context of the business. Without confidence in one's data, BI brings little value to the decision-making process.

Purpose-built Services

This layer provides the meat of the solution suite. It contains the query, reporting, dashboard, scorecard, event detection, and other functions that users will apply to the data available to them. For example, a report should be capable of being created on any and all data sources. There should be no difference in accessing a relational data source or an OLAP cube for reporting.

Reporting and Analytics

To address much of the "Why?" question mentioned earlier, Cognos 8 offers a rich set of reporting and analysis functions (Fig. 3.5). It is very important to be able to convey this information in a wide variety of ways. Different users interpret data in different ways. Whereas one may find a detailed, graphic report meaningful, another may prefer a graph or chart. Placement on the user's output display (screen, printed report, browser, etc.) should be highly customizable.

Why?

- **Enterprise Reporting**
  - Supports multiple report types: Production, Managed, Ad-hoc, Financial, etc.
  - Is adaptable to any data source
  - Operates from a single metadata layer
  - Can be personalized and targeted
  - Can be distributed via email, portal, MS-Office, search application, and mobile device

- **Analysis**
  - Enables the guided exploration of information that pertains to all dimensions of your business
  - Performs complex analysis and scenario modeling easily and quickly
  - Gets to the "why" behind an event or action to improve business performance
  - Moves from summary level to detail levels of information effortlessly

Figure 3.5: Addressing the "why?" factor

IBM Cognos reporting capabilities are second to none. It is possible to deliver "pixel-perfect" output to an end user in a wide variety of output types and formats. The reporting layer offers different levels of function based upon the user's skill level and re-quirements. It provides an easy-to-use, intuitive interface with a full set of help, tutorials, and end-user assists to make the reporting tasks as easy to engage and complete as possible.

Using Cognos, it is easy to define drillable reports and charts that permit users to obtain more complete information about a particular result. Problem-solving most often involves beginning with a particular metric or value and probing further. One of the most appeal-ing features of OLAP systems is the ability to drill, slice, and dissect data at various levels.

The IBM Cognos analysis option supports a wide variety of OLAP sources such as Cognos PowerPlay, Cognos TM1, Oracle/Hyperion Essbase, MS Analysis Services, SAP BW, and IBM's Cubing Services (ROLAP) feature of DB2. Thus, the adherence to open standards is upheld, offering analysis features and functions to the broadest set of users in the industry.

Dashboards and Scorecards

Measuring and Monitoring - How Are We Doing?

- **Dashboards**
  - Translate complex information into high-impact presentations
  - Allow you to spot changes
  - Are highly intuitive
  - Align decision makers

- **Scorecards**
  - Provide instantaneous measurement relative to targets and benchmarks
  - Align decisions and tactics with strategic initiatives
  - Support scorecarding methodologies
  - Ensure ownership aand accountability

Figure 3.6: Dashboards and scorecards

Event Detection and Actions

Much of the success in crafting a BI/PM solution lies in the appropriate delivery of information to users at a time when it is needed and in the context of their role within the organization.

Certain users will be concerned only about the existence of a particular value or the occurrence of a particular event. Cognos 8 provides a powerful and user-defined event/trigger capability. It may well be that a particular set of users only requires information if some specific event has occurred; otherwise their involvement in BI processes is minimal. In case an event triggers a response, these users may be notified in a variety of ways, such as via e-mail or by sending output to a personal digital assistant (PDA) device. If the critical event does not occur or all is well, they don't want to be bothered.

The Presentation Layer

Once the user has created some BI/PM output, how do she wish to view the results? IBM Cognos 8 is based upon thin-client architecture, but results may be provided in a number of output types and styles. Output may be routed back to a browser, a PDA, a PDF file, or an Excel spreadsheet, or imbedded within a process such as an e-mail.

Different users may require the same output in varying formats (Fig. 3.7). The IBM Cognos 8 infrastructure is such that a result only needs to be produced once, but can served up in a variety of forms and formats. Output to Excel alone has proven to be of tremendous value, such that the underlying data and results are easily refreshed and pushed to a sheet with all formats and styles intact. This allows the spreadsheet to be autonomous, and free from the requirements of maintaining the data.

Flexible Access to Information

* Any language (robust Unicode support)

* Any format (PDF, HTML, Excel, XML...)

* Self-service access with personal alerts and search-based authoring and exploration

* Automated delivery with scheduling, email bursting, and event-triggers

* Access from within applications; in-process

* Access in location that best suits the user (MS Office, mobile devices, search...)

Figure 3.7: Flexible access to information

Using IBM Cognos 8, the user can access any and all data in the organization's infrastructure. She can customize the user interface to accommodate her personal linguistic requirements, skill level, required functions, output styles, and formats, and she can automate many of these processes.

Planning, Budgeting, and Forecasting

So far, we have the "Why?" questions well covered. Now we need to look at the "What should we be doing?" aspect of effective BI and PM. For this we recommend Cognos Planning, Budgeting, and Forecasting, which allows the user to look ahead at scenarios that should be considered. This part of the Cognos portfolio warrants an entire book in its own right, but we'll try to articulate the value and impact of proper planning, budgeting, and forecasting in these few paragraphs.

Leading companies routinely address planning obstacles and improve their processes. They take advantage of new technologies and employ best practices to be maximally effective. Their reward comes in the form of more accurate plans, more timely forecasts and reforecasts, and more effective decision-making. Corporate decision-makers typically voice similar concerns about planning, budgeting, and forecasting:

- Processes are tedious and time-consuming.

- Data integrity is questionable.

- The explanation of variances is difficult.

- Existing tools are inflexible and do not support a dynamic environment.

Despite the massive investments to implement ERP systems in the last decade or so, most planning is still performed using spreadsheets, e-mail, and countless staff hours. This proves costly in the long run, as spreadsheets are simply not designed to effectively support these processes. Inhibitors include:

- Business rules (formulas) are mixed with data and prone to corruption.

- Frequent file-swapping occurs among users, and cross-organization teams find it difficult to work in tandem.

- Presenting and analyzing data from different perspectives is difficult.

- Data aggregation is difficult and time-consuming.

- The business model is not represented well . . . if at all.

- Complex calculations, multidimensional reporting, and analysis are nearly impossible.

So, how does the IBM Cognos portfolio address these concerns and issues? Based upon its TM1 database, IBM Cognos provides a set of tools and interfaces that allow an organization to separate business rules, logic, complex calculations, and aggregations from the data. It also provides a set of pre-built, best-practice templates to minimize risk and accelerate time to business value.

The IBM Cognos planning, budgeting, and forecasting applications provide a lean infrastructure that allows the organization to plan and re-plan quickly (Fig. 3.8). It is provided as a web-based application, thus offering collaborative efforts to be deployed easily and globally.

Enterprise planning, budgeting, and forecasting from IBM Cognos lets Finance departments create and maintain models for thousands of tightly linked operations. These planning models can be created and communicated in days, not months. Cutting the time spent on budgeting and planning processes gives decision-makers more time for in-depth analysis, so that Finance can be a better partner to the business.

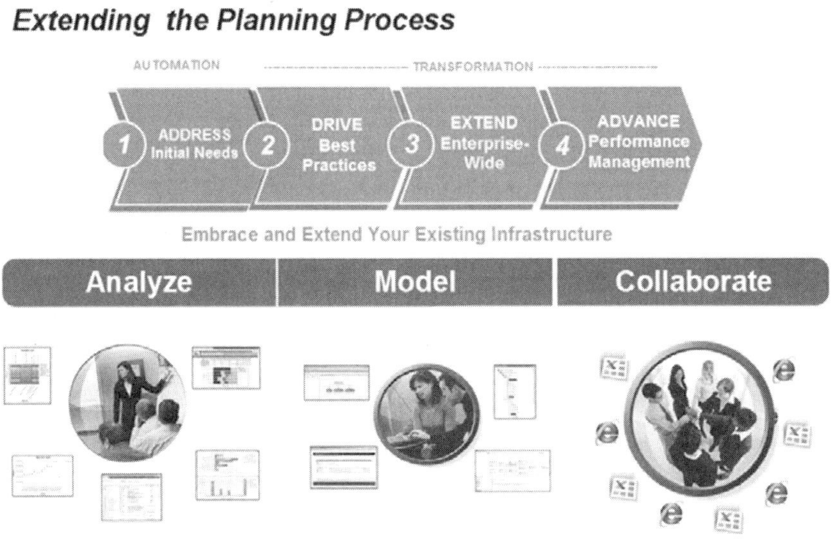

Figure 3.8: Extending the planning process

Developing and delivering a more global, adept planning process is a means to dynamically changing the effectiveness of the business. The IBM Cognos suite offers the following benefits to any organization:

- Integrated, strategic, operational, and financial planning reside in one system.

- Collaborative, web-based planning enables participation at any time from anywhere.

- Simplified version control allows frequent reforecasting and execution of what-if scenarios.

- Data is kept up to date, due to the user's ability to directly add to or modify a central planning database.

- Efficiency is increased as finance managers and departmental managers spend less time managing data.

- Customized views and formulas allow all business drivers to be contained within the system.

- Accuracy is increased, based upon a common plan with fewer broken links, fresher data, and more accurate rollups.

- The decision-making process is led by Finance.

Collaboration and Effective Communication

One aspect of BI and PM that has dramatically changed of late is how the results and impact of information are conveyed. After we have uncovered answers to one or more of the critical business problems affecting us, how do we utilize this information in a collaborative manner?

IBM Cognos 8 provides a rich set of operations that integrate well with MS Office, enterprise portals, mashups, and more. It allows the rapid communication of BI/PM results among users globally. The term often used is *actionable results*. As we continue our journey to enable a Smarter Planet, being able to quickly share information and form a consensus with our peers, domain experts, and others is essential to our infrastructure.

Even when information is timely and accurate, there is no guarantee that it will be interpreted properly or acted upon in a timely manner. By extending IBM Cognos 8 with collaboration functions, a business can set the stage for effective communications and peer-to-peer discussions. Having a common metadata layer provides consistency as well as control of information throughout the organization.

Having a common interface also allows for flexibility as individuals move around within an organization. Once a corporate BI standard has been set, people within the organization begin to share a common user experience. Skills increase at all levels as the known paradigm of how the tool works becomes part of the organization's "DNA." Having a set of commonly used functions (e.g., event notification and collaboration) drives consistent communication throughout.

Portal Interactions

IBM Cognos 8 can be driven through a variety of portal interfaces, including one that ships with the product in case the customer does not have a standard in place. It is possible to place numerous BI/PM objects on the glass at the same time. All of these objects (e.g., reports) may present information from different data sources and/or systems. Rather than looking at information from disparate systems individually, it is now common to deliver a dashboard to the user that contains a wealth of information germane to his needs.

End users can create their own dashboards rather than wait for an IT specialist to deliver their personalized version. This extends the concept of effective communication to a new level.

It is possible to "wire" systems together at the portal interface level, such as having a value from a report on one system drive a query on another. This approach often allows collaboration and cross-referencing that would have required a full system rewrite. This approach opens the door to solving complex business questions heretofore impossible to address.

The Data Dilemma: From Structured to Unstructured

Earlier, we mentioned the untrammeled growth of data both within an organization and externally. Effective analysis of data held in an organization's internal systems, typically contained in structured (database) formats, is a challenge in and of itself. A user must be able to access DB2, Oracle, SAP, Informix, VSAM, IMS, and a variety of other sources and formats. Added to that are the numerous OLAP engines, with their own data stores and formats, and the emergence of new, semi-structured formats such as XML. All these must be accessible from a BI/PM platform. There's also a strong requirement to address the global information directory contained within the Internet.

A quick web search reveals some startling statistics on data generation. The estimated current growth of data is 15 petabytes (each petabyte is 1,000 terabytes or 10^{15} bytes or 1,024 terabytes) added every single day. This staggering increase in data volume and potential end users will continue to expand on a global basis.

Not all data that gets dumped onto the world stage is relevant or pertinent to a business's process—the problem lies in the fact that so much *may* be of importance, but how does one slog through it all to pick out the gems?

IBM Cognos 8 provides access to data held in a huge variety of formats, including unstructured information. Integration with IBM's Text Analytics software extends the reach into the myriad data sources held in notes, documents, web pages, and more.

It is possible to render unstructured information into structured analyses, where answers to a problem may come from a source unknown prior to performing this transition, such as competitive information published externally that contains recent product market figures and more. You cannot ignore the need to access any data that may be available to your users from any source.

IBM Cognos Go! Search: Enterprise Search

IBM Cognos has invested heavily in search technologies and is able to deliver highly filtered and ranked information from internal as well as external data. For example, using Go! Search (Fig. 3.9), a user could search a library of known reports and find those reports he didn't remember the name of or those he wanted to identify by content, or to simply see what others may have created.

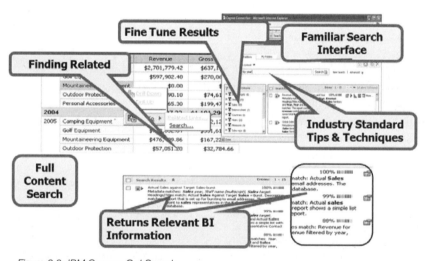

Figure 3.9: IBM Cognos Go! Search

In a broader context, if the user wants to search a vast sea of unstructured information (e.g., the Internet) and return possible interesting subjects or those deserving further investigation, IBM Cognos Go! Search allows for that as well.

IBM Cognos Go! Search offers significant value to customers:

- A full-content and pre-indexed BI search solution out of the box and *without requiring any third-party product installs*:
  - » 73% of end users believe full-content searching on BI is important (IBM Cognos Survey).

- IBM Cognos has *technology integration,* not just partnerships involving the leaders in search, including IBM, Autonomy, and Google.

- Support is provided for industry-standard tips and techniques, such as phrases, Boolean logic, and stemming.

- Pre-indexing of BI content delivers instant results.

- It is possible to find related leveraging contextual information, and full-content search allows users to find the most relevant related BI content.

- Search for all BI content is possible, including cubes, metrics, scorecards, events, and packages, as well as reports and dashboards.

Industry estimates often cite that roughly 85% of the information held electronically is contained in unstructured or semi-structured format. Internal information may be held in documents, images, e-mails, and more; the Internet and other unstructured sources also must be factored into an organization's view of "its data." Because any one piece of this data may hold valuable information pertinent to your business, Cognos helps you find the relevant information in these sources and make sense of it.

Business Intelligence User Segmentation

It is terribly naïve to assume that all end users can be effective with a BI tool and that they all have similar needs and skills. More and more, however, there is a huge demand for self-service BI/PM. IBM Cognos provides a wide array of supported end-user types. For example, for a less-skilled, more casual user, it offers a lighter, less functional user option. If the user is a skilled professional with a tendency to explore data and develop sophisticated analyses, then he can be provided with a more robust suite of functions.

BI/PM tools are far less effective when simply thrown at the end-user population in a large, complex bundle. Varying skills and requirements dictate a need to provide segmentation of function that addresses specific user types. To provide this wide array of functional choice, IBM Cognos 8 provides the ability to dole out features and functions according to an individual's needs.

In the realm of BI/PM, it is quite common for a set of end users to be primary providers to others. It could be that they have more technical skill or a deeper knowledge regarding certain business processes that others can take advantage of. Cognos 8's rich output functions and depth of analysis provides a palette that the producers of BI/PM output can modify to convey results to their constituency.

User Segmentation for Effective Deployment

There are many instances of organizations investing in a large number of seat licenses because they received a very good price point, only to find their ability to deploy is severely limited. Sometimes this is due to the fact that there simply is no plan; sometimes it's because the ability to deliver the proper functional level to end users was not granular enough.

IBM Cognos 8 assumes that end users and communities have a varying set of skills and requirements. Typically, there will be far more casual users and basic consumers than highly skilled individuals. But all users, regardless of ability, need to work from a common set of data.

A complete set of administration functions is provided that allows the administrator to mete out or adjust the amount of function consumed by end users. Along with the ability to restrict the functions available, the number of options and features provided in the user interface are allocated accordingly.

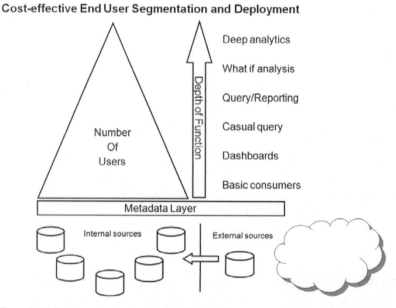

Figure 3.10: End-user deployment by functional ability

In Figure 3.10, we see the typical pyramid of end users and their relative ability to utilize BI/PM functions. The categories of functions are merely illustrative of a range of functions, not all-encompassing. The important point is that we have an open architecture with access to all the information needed to make solid business decisions. The user community is provided as much or as little function as needed or required.

Effective use of the BI/PM portfolio, as well as confidence in the underpinning data, are contained within this platform. Whether an end user is reviewing a simple report or receiving results from a peer with deep analytic skills, their mutual confidence is assured.

Cross-pollination across the organization is also enhanced because this deployment has removed data silos, at least at the logical level. Business users are now segmented by skills and need to access information, not by where they sit or by a narrow BI solution silo.

Systems Management and Service-level Agreements

IBM Cognos 8 offers a full complement of administration and systems management capabilities to be responsive to changes in users, user profiles, and to monitor system resources. It is quick and easy to identify problem areas such as processes that are causing bottlenecks or taking excessive resources.

Many users of BI/PM tools and functions are simply investigating the information they have been given. Some may access small amounts of data, while others may produce enormous queries. In ad hoc environments, it is essential to understand the user community and be able to address variable usage patterns. No one ever intends to perform inefficient, excessive work on a BI system . . . sometimes it just happens. Without effective administration and monitoring tools, a BI solution is nearly impossible to manage. With Cognos administrative tools it is easy to:

- Define users, groups, resources

- Alter a user's profile to access or turn off various Cognos 8 components

- Define data access and/or limitations

- Monitor system usage and resources

- Get a clear picture of overall system use, load balancing, etc.

Business Intelligence Standardization

One major trend we see is careful scrutiny of an organization's BI portfolio. Many clients tell us that they have a set of tools from various vendors, many of which have overlapping functions. Many of these offerings have not been effectively deployed and, as a result, there is no one standard BI tool in the enterprise.

The implications of this scenario are many, but one of the greatest impacts upon an organization with multiple, fragmented tools is that there is far less opportunity to share skills and results. Many BI tools have been acquired over a period of time, and each one will have some pocket of expertise within the organization. Over time, these tools exhibit limitations and possible shortcomings as an enterprise expands its Information Agenda and these technologies do not keep pace.

To standardize on a reduced set of BI/PM tools often requires sweeping change in how an organization operates. One of the first and potentially greatest steps to take is the establishment of a *Center of Competency* (CoC) for BI/PM.

The CoC is a centralized organization whose mission is to be the focal point for all tool evaluation, training, deployment, monitoring, and management. By centralizing the oversight of BI/PM efforts, a consistent environment is established for more effective use of resources. Users have an internal group invested in their success and available to help them decide the best options to addressing their BI/PM needs.

When a business decides to move forward with a BI standardization agenda, some regulatory body must be in place to help overcome objections, as well as to assist in the adoption of a new or different tool should other tools be targeted for sunsetting.

A CoC is better equipped to assess vendor offerings and match them to requirements across the organization. The skills and internal business knowledge acquired then can be shared and applied in several business areas.

Another very important factor in going with a BI standardization agenda is selecting the proper tool/platform, which must be able to perform all the functions that are being replaced as the number of offerings is pared down. The IBM Cognos portfolio we've been reviewing has only been lightly touched upon, and many more products and functions can easily be found on IBM's many web sites. We feel confident, however, that the portfolio we've outlined here delivers all the functional capability and business value required within an enterprise.

However, one last aspect needs to be covered: What about performance? Can you really deploy IBM Cognos to hundreds, thousands, tens of thousands of users throughout the enterprise and provide the speed, size, and scale you need?

Performance and Scalability

To effectively deliver enterprise-ready BI/PM solutions, IBM has performed extensive testing and benchmarks to make sure Cognos 8 scales in a linear and consistent manner. Testing has been performed on several platforms. The results are available on demand and can be obtained on request, or you can perform a simple search on the web and see the sites where this information is available.

Liner scalability is absolutely essential to delivering effective and efficient BI/PM solutions. In our testing, we varied mixes of end users, databases, query loads, and many system parameters to see if Cognos can deliver documentation on proven practices that will make your business more productive and faster.

Testing demonstrated IBM Cognos 8 BI scales linearly to large user groups.

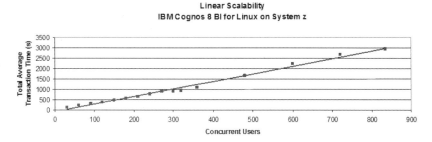

Linear Scalability
IBM Cognos 8 BI for Linux on System z

Testing was conducted with up to **90,000 named users**

Figure 3.11: Scalability testing with IBM Cognos 8 on Linux for System z

The newest addition to the IBM Cognos 8 portfolio is that for Linux on System z. Like its predecessor platforms, we tested IBM Cognos 8 BI running on this platform with the same, consistent linear scaling results (Fig. 3.11).

50TB Study

This study may be of particular interest in that it was primarily targeted at delivering an operational BI infrastructure. Operational BI is an emerging area where one is delivering real-time information to BI users, such as customer service representatives. If you refer back to the pyramid in Figure 3.10, note that, at the base, we see a larger number of casual end users.

These users are not sophisticated, tend to use BI in an imbedded manner, and receive small answer sets from large volumes of data. The assumption in this test series was that each user would be querying a different part of the database, so we made sure that we did not cache results or reuse queries, to accurately reflect an operational BI scenario. As in all previous testing we performed, the behavior of Cognos was consistent and the scale measurements were linear.

IBM uses Cognos suite to deliver BI/PM results to its employees worldwide, using one set of application services for an employee base in excess of 47,000 end users. They are often asked if they utilize their own technologies to their benefit. The answer here is a clear "yes."

Summary

An effective BI/PM solution is only as good as the underlying infrastructure of information capture, process, and flow. It must provide end users with a rich set of functions that fall within their skills level and manner of usage. To provide this set of requirements, IBM has developed and delivered an entire suite of products and functions that interoperate and integrate in a modern SOA platform.

BI/PM solutions must interlock and share a common set of metadata, where all end users understand the data, its definitions, and have confidence in its accuracy and timeliness. IT confidence grows as it finds it is capable of responding rapidly to changes and additions in data. With Cognos 8, IT knows it has helped end users select the proper BI/PM tools to be more adept at addressing the ever-changing world of information and technology.

Corporate confidence in infrastructure grows as well, as the issues of data volume, lack of confidence and agility, and multiple versions of the truth are addressed. Success is measured by enhanced business value and increased use of the system. User confidence grows and increased deployment occurs, accompanied by the feeling that, "We got it right this time; we're getting the information we need."

The concept of a "Smarter Planet" is not a clever marketing slogan; it is an initiative that acknowledges the fact that, globally, we are all interconnected as never before. As this connected and global community expands, the issues surrounding the volume of information and its new sources will increase beyond our wildest dreams. The need to put it into a meaningful context for interpretation has never been greater.

Now let's take a look what is required to build an effective information infrastructure to support the new intelligence applications.

4

Building the Information Infrastructure

Information can be analyzed to expose a world of valuable opportunities, but if you are not confident in the data that was analyzed, you may be reticent to act. Without action based on the insights derived from the data, decisions become intuitive or opinion-based, and are frequently flawed.

Can You Act with Confidence in Your Information?

Finding, gathering, and integrating information is a critical aspect of New Intelligence initiatives. The value of information depends, first and foremost, on whether or not business users trust it. Simply collecting data without understanding its meaning or level of accuracy will result in information that is unsuitable for decision making. Organizations commonly have at least some degree of inconsistent, incomplete, and incorrect information that makes it useable for daily operations but not for analytics.

Many projects have failed or have been significantly delayed because data was simply "thrown over the wall" into a warehouse without appropriately addressing these issues.

Organizations can achieve trusted information through a systematic approach to information integration that goes beyond copying data, to include aspects of understanding the information and resolving inconsistencies. Every day, managers from different lines of business meet to discuss various aspects of a business, such as the company's revenues and profit margin; they all have "the numbers," but all the numbers are different. Nobody has the wrong numbers; they are all just various perspectives of discrete areas of the business, not a single, coordinated view that sees the company as a whole. These various perspectives may contain unrecognized revenue or fail to include certain chargebacks.

How do organizations ensure that everyone in the business is more informed, more engaged, and aligned in decision-making, so that their decisions drive better business outcomes? Without the right information, employees revert to either intuition or inaction,

neither of which are acceptable. Organizations recognize that they need to deliver relevant data when and where its needed, and they need to deliver it from fragmented, disparate systems and at the volume and velocity required to create *trusted information.*

The Challenge

Historically, businesses have often underestimated the complexity of building integrated and trusted information. Most business performance management, analytics, and warehousing initiatives that oversimplified or neglected information integration, equating it with "just copying data" have failed. To guarantee a positive return on investment for any information integration solution, users must have enough confidence in the information to be able to act decisively when opportunities arise. This chapter reviews the process of gaining confidence in enterprise data by capitalizing on the tools and capabilities of IBM's InfoSphere offerings (Fig. 4.1).

Driving Business Confidence Into Your Information

Improving business confidence in information is generally focused around three main areas:

- *Information understanding* through increased context and consistency of definition

- *Information trust* by managing the quality of the data and improving its quality over time

- *Information reach* to all required data when it is needed, with a full range of delivery strategies

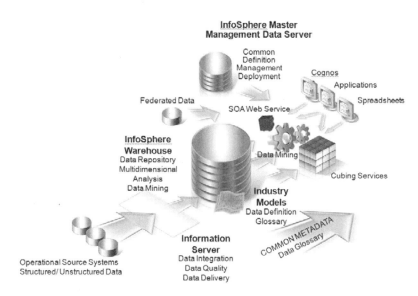

Figure 4.1: InfoSphere Portfolio — End-to-End Integration

Information Understanding

The first and most important challenge is ensuring that the requirements and expectations from the business side are aligned with the design and implementation on the IT side. Business and IT users often speak different languages and lack the organizational structures, methodology, and technology to address these differences through improved communication and collaboration.

You will struggle to communicate unless both parties agree on the definition of the words they are using. Misunderstandings caused by incorrect interpretation of enterprise information increases the risk of expensive errors. The complete business costs of ambiguous information are even more dramatic. Productivity plummets when executives in the boardroom or employees on the stock floor waste time searching for or misinterpreting poorly labeled data. Unclear information can cripple a sales force, obscure opportunities, and slow response times to shifts in market conditions. For example; a retailer may state that the daily store sales for store 39 is $125,342.43. But what does that mean? Does the amount include or exclude returns? The returns may make a significant difference in this number, and may substantially affect a decision about that store.

Unfortunately, it is all too common for business and IT experts to interpret the same business term in different ways. The same thing happens between various lines of business. For example, it is relatively easy to get multiple lines of business to agree that they need customer information. What is often considerably more difficult is gaining agreement across these groups as to what constitutes a customer. At what point in time does an entity become a customer, and then when do they stop being a customer? The term "customer" may seem so obvious that it is never clearly defined, even though different types of customers exist (e.g., prospects versus current clients versus past clients). These are very basic issues, but must be addressed if all business players are to be "on the same page."

Even worse, these conversations sometimes never take place at all, because a lack of precision in business terms hides the fact that a fundamental disagreement exists. When the meanings of critical business terms, such as elements in a report, are not clearly defined by the business, IT teams may not realize this ambiguity and may make inappropriate architectural decisions based on their incorrect assumptions.

Many businesses are moving aggressively to counter data ambiguity by building a *common business vocabulary* or business glossary—an authoritative dictionary of business terms and relationships used across an enterprise (Fig. 4.2). Designed to be used by any employee, the business glossary defines the terms used in everyday communication, such as e-mail requests for business intelligence reports, marketing plans, legal documentation, and communication with customers. In addition, IT professionals employ the glossary content to ensure that a proper, common language is used when designing the IT infrastructure, applications, and reports. A business glossary can connect workers across the enterprise to critical business information they can trust, helping to eliminate the misunderstandings that cause lost time, lost opportunities, and lost revenue.

Understand: Establish the Working Vocabulary

You Cannot Communicate Unless both Parties Understand the Words

Figure 4.2: The business glossary

Organizations cannot really address the challenge of a common vocabulary simply by defining business terms without ensuring that the vocabulary is commonly accepted across business and IT. A common vocabulary also must be managed to avoid unapproved changes that alter meanings unintentionally. For example, one line of business cannot simply declare that a "prospect" is equivalent to a "customer." Effective *stewardship* is therefore a critical success factor in developing a common vocabulary.

Data stewardship ensures that the appropriate organizational structures and processes are in place to coordinate the definition of terms and control their accuracy.

Another challenge is how to achieve *ubiquity of the common business vocabulary*. It is not enough to just load a large group of terms and definitions into a dictionary and believe the problem is solved; these definitions must be proliferated across the organization and made common to every user's vocabulary. That means the vocabulary must be accessible within the normal work and tool environment of business users, as well as IT personnel. As Figure 4.2 illustrates, we have a reoccurring processes of identifying and growth.

Based on this business glossary, we must then derive a logical perspective of the business concepts, their properties, and how they relate to each other. Ideally, this logical model extends to a full understanding of the business processes and other consumers that rely on this information. This model then provides a detailed understanding of the contexts within which information is used and further enables us to converge on reusable definitions of information structures across the enterprise.

Data Models

An effective way to accelerate a project is to start with a data model that has all the required business and technical terms. IBM Industry Data Models provide a blueprint for data integration projects. An essential component of any data warehouse infrastructure—and the key to breaking down information silos—is a data model that specifies how data is structured and how it is accessed for analysis and reporting. The model provides technical and business data definitions that become the blueprint for a successful data warehouse. Traditional data warehouses are often built upon homegrown or application-specific data models that fall short of dynamic data warehousing requirements. However, using the IBM approach, companies establish an enterprise-wide data model to avoid a situation in which new applications disrupt existing applications as data is redefined.

One of the most frustrating obstacles to successful business decision making is the lack of consistency. With no agreement on data terms and definitions, there are multiple answers to the same question. Calculating revenue, costs, and liabilities all require consistent business rules and terms to allow the data to be understood in context and enable fact-based decision-making.

The primary obstacle in achieving a holistic view of the organization centers on the absence of an enterprise data model. This is a model of the unified business, across all of its silos of operational systems. It is a glossary of terms and definitions that defines the business and its processes. Many organizations have attempted to build enterprise models and some have been successful, but many have failed due to a deficient understanding of the key applications and metrics that the business requires going forward. Building a data warehouse without an enterprise model is like building a house without a set of building plans. The results can be very expensive and can result in a schedule of endless iterations and modification that try to accommodate new functionality.

As Figure 4.3 shows, IBM has six industry Enterprise Data Models with numerous dimensional models to address the unique issues of each industry. The dimensional models enable in-depth analysis of a given subject, such as profitability.

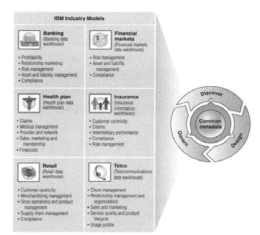

Figure 4.3: IBM industry Enterprise Data Models

Data Profiling

The next step is analyzing and understanding the sources of information. Does the data really conform to the semantic and structural definition defined? Do any integrity constraint violations exist? What problems should we expect when integrating the data due to poor quality? The requirement to address such issues is commonly referred to as the need for *data profiling*. Data profiling is defined as a specific technique or process, usually automated, to statistically measure and infer data content and relationships based on the actual underlying data, as well as to validate the data against technical and business rules. This information will be critical in assessing the viability of the data and the level of effort needed to cleanse the data in subsequent steps. IBM addresses this need with the Information Analyzer.

Traceability and Auditability

To truly understand a data item, a user must understand its root, ancestry, or linage. How was this data derived? Was it a direct feed from a store, an output from an application in accounting, or a forecasting application in sales? Is this database the system where the information originates (e.g., through data entry), or has this system been populated through another data source? The identification of the ultimate origin of the information, its path from one database to another, and the type of operations between them strongly influences the trust users have in the information. Often, the same entity exists in multiple systems with inconsistent information; for example, the same customer has different addresses depending on which system is accessed. *Data lineage analysis* helps identify where information comes from and determine whether it can be trusted or needs to be further validated, cleansed, or transformed. By identifying the source of the original data and what transformations have occurred to the data, the user can quickly assess its relevance to a given issue.

In addition, to fully understand data, a user must have the ability to trace and audit her data (Fig. 4.4). To be able to determine each functional change that has occurred to the data, every sort, blend, filter, or calculation that has been performed on the data must be known. Ideally, this capability is coupled with impact analysis, enabling developers to understand the impact to each application that uses the data if the definition of the data were to change.

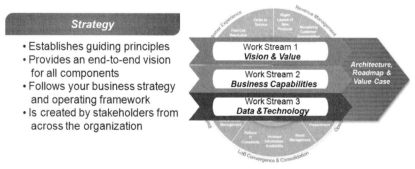

Figure 4.4: Data must be traceable and auditable

Database Inventory

Another area that requires tight collaboration between business and IT is the identification of repositories and databases that contain relevant information. Once these data sources have been found, business analysts can identify the relevant elements in them and, at a high level, can identify how they map to the new integrated structures of the business analytic solution. Business users need better tooling support than simplistic spreadsheets to specify these mappings in a format that is not too technical but lets them collaborate with the IT community. Although the use of spreadsheets for this task is common, it is also problematic.

Because spreadsheets are not linked to the actual underlying systems, elements are often missing or incorrectly specified. Even if the information is correct, copying it into data integration tools is frequently a manual and labor-intensive task. Organizations need a tool that supports the business-driven specification of mappings and the generation of technical artifacts from these specifications.

Finally, like any corporate asset, data needs to be inventoried.

- Which data is managed by which system?
- What relationships exist between data in different systems?
- How do I map data together for new uses?
- What should my data look like to allow me to use it to optimize my business?
- How does the business use the data?
- What meaning does it have to the business?
- Which systems are best sources for specific pieces of information?
- What data quality issues do I have?

IBM's Business Glossary, the Metadata Workbench that comes with each of the major components, and Information Server provide this functionality. In addition, Glossary Anywhere can enable the pervasive use of glossary terms by providing the agreed-upon definition of any term in any PC desktop application.

Foundation Tools

The Business Glossary, Information Analyzer, Industry Data Models, and Metadata Workbench are four of IBM's InfoSphere Foundation Tools (Fig. 4.5) that help companies establish a data governance environment. The InfoSphere Foundation Tools help organizations build their information-led projects with an integrated set of tooling designed to bring business and IT teams together with better results. The toolkit is part of the larger IBM InfoSphere Information Server software portfolio, which enables organizations to maintain data quality over time, manage accessibility and structure, and deliver information to the systems and decision-makers that need it.

InfoSphere Foundation Tools provide a unique combination of capabilities to help organizations define and manage their data. The tools help organizations discover and categorize new information sources, model and map data schemas, create business rules, establish and maintain data stewardship, manage business vocabulary and relationship hierarchies, and centralize this information in a shared repository to facilitate active collaboration between business and IT. The Foundation tools are the basic set of tools to begin the process of data governance, which will be discussed in Chapter 5.

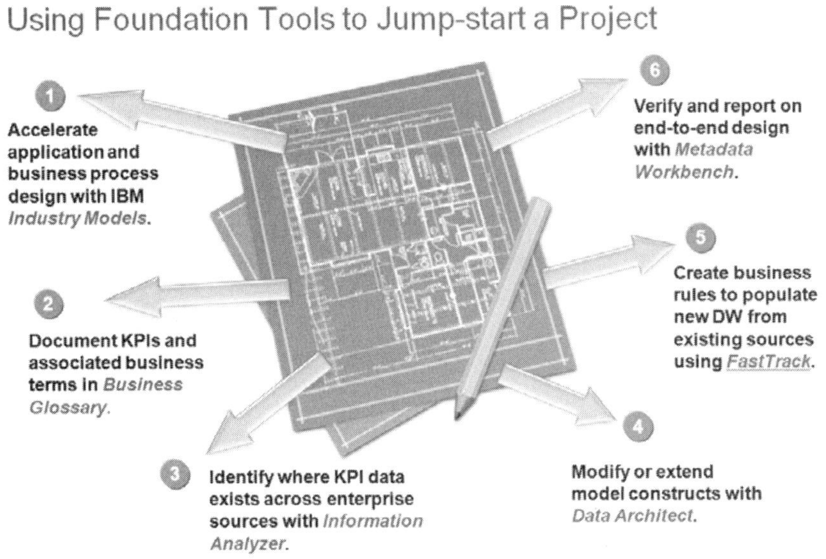

Using Foundation Tools to Jump-start a Project

1 Accelerate application and business process design with IBM *Industry Models*.

2 Document KPIs and associated business terms in *Business Glossary*.

3 Identify where KPI data exists across enterprise sources with *Information Analyzer*.

4 Modify or extend model constructs with *Data Architect*.

5 Create business rules to populate new DW from existing sources using *FastTrack*.

6 Verify and report on end-to-end design with *Metadata Workbench*.

Figure 4.5: Foundation Tools

As part of defining an information strategy, implementers need to first align their goals with senior management's business objectives. The information system must be capable of supporting business-driving metrics and able to monitor Key Performance Indictors (KPIs). To deliver on this requirement, a blueprint is required to guide the implementer through the steps of implementation. The Foundation Tools provide the components to guide the project through each of its steps.

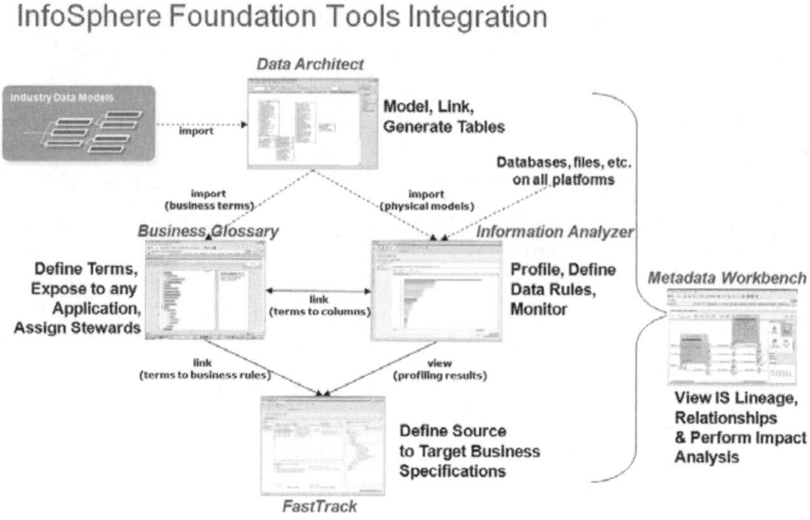

InfoSphere Foundation Tools Integration

Figure 4.6: Integrated InfoSphere Foundation Tools

Figure 4.6 illustrates how each of the Foundation Tools complements the functions of the prior tool while maintaining its common information in the Metadata Workbench. This enables a high degree of reuse, plus the ability to automate many manual functions that frequently absorb a large portion of project's resources.

Information Trust

Information can only support trusted, timely, and effective decision making if users have a high confidence in its accuracy. Trusted data is correct, complete, and consistent across the enterprise. Information cannot be successfully connected if it doesn't meet fundamental requirements such as alignment of keys, availability of critical information, and consistency of data in its fields. Data quality issues, especially if they go unidentified, pose a serious risk to obtaining accurate answers from the data. At a minimum, they impact the value of the information being delivered because it will be incorrect or incomplete. In the worst case, the information might be so poor that any use of it is impossible.

Data Profiling

As we have already discussed, using Information Analyzer to profile source data for an information-led project is an effective way to gain understanding of that source data. To develop trust in this data, it must be analyzed and corrected. Fields must contain the appropriate information, and all of the interlocking keys must be validated. The objective at this step is to perform these activities with as much automation as possible, reusing information that was previously captured and addressing any issues that were presented.

Data Cleansing

To address the data quality problems identified through data profiling, the data must be cleansed or corrected. Many organizations acknowledge that their current information has data quality issues. Unless the business addresses these issues, business performance management applications will not provide correct information. Consider the example of a company that wants to analyze customer profitability across multiple, currently isolated product lines. If the customer data (e.g., address information) is not cleansed and standardized, duplicate and incorrect information will negatively impact the result. If the same customer has two different addresses in two product-line databases, this customer cannot be identified as the same customer, and the analysis will lead to incorrect results — namely, the assumption that no joint customers exist across product lines. This requirement for *data cleansing* includes the standardization of data (e.g., to establish addresses with the same format), the enrichment of information (e.g., through adding missing postal codes in addresses), and the removal of duplicates. The data quality continuum includes data profiling, standardization, matching, and monitoring—and IBM Information Server delivers them all.

In almost every survey of data warehouse failures, the lack of data quality is usually one of the top three reasons for the project failing to meet its objectives. But how can data be so flawed when it is used by the operational systems? There are three reasons:

1. The data is focused at a specific task.

2. The data is good enough to meet that need.

3. The context of data creation is different from data use.

When data is captured in an operational system, it is captured for a specific purpose. Many application databases contain additional fields that carry extra information that would be valuable to the business, but are not used in the everyday process. Therefore, the fields' data values are not monitored and managed as closely as the data required to drive the application, and often contain values that are inexplicable, inaccurate, or arbitrary. In addition, fields may be reused for special issues, resulting in completely foreign information residing in a field, relative to the data description.

The second reason is that the data is good enough to meet the need of that application, but not good enough for use on a broader basis. For example, a customer's name and address may be good enough for the post office to be able to deliver a statement, but is not good enough to easily merge the multiple relationships the customer has with the organization.

To gain trusted data in the warehouse, organizations must analyze, understand, and profile the source data that will be loaded into the warehouse. They must standardize the terms and semantically blend the data into a format that can be consumed by the required tools and applications. In addition, the process needs to leave a trail of information to document where the data originated and which transformations occurred to the data. But the issue of trusted data is not a static one. Consider: The US Postal Serve states that over 40 million Americans move annually, which means that, on average, one-sixth of an organization's customer base changes addresses each year.

Input must be cleansed to identify, correct, match, standardize, and reconcile inaccurate or redundant data. Data cleansing capabilities help ensure auditable data quality and consistency by standardizing, validating, matching, and merging data to create comprehensive and authoritative information. By improving the quality of information, IBM Information Server can help boost user confidence, facilitate efficient and effective business decisions, improve customer individualization, help identify revenue-generating opportunities, and assemble the auditable, trusted information needed to comply with regulations such as the Sarbanes-Oxley Act and Basel II.

Integrating and Transforming Information

In most business performance management and warehousing initiatives, the information is not already available as required by the business. Instead, it is spread over multiple heterogeneous systems, in different formats, and often even with conflicting values. Even where data quality is not an issue, the conflicting needs of operational and analytical environments require the extraction of business information into a form that is suitable for analytical applications. One of the most fundamental challenges of information integration is how to bridge this gap. How can we use the existing information and transform and integrate it so that it can be delivered to business users in the form they need? Legacy systems often were designed and introduced when business-user requirements were quite different from today. These systems continue to play an important role because they still manage some of the most important information assets in an enterprise. Often, they cannot simply be replaced just because business users need a new way to look at information or want to combine information differently. We need *data transformation* and *data cleansing* capabilities to extract information from information sources; transform, aggregate, and cleanse it; and load it into a warehouse for consumption by business applications.

Complicating the task of data transformation is the potentially very large volumes of data (e.g., all the financial information from a large worldwide company) and the need to process that information in a relatively short period of time. Extracting information from existing operational systems often negatively affects performance, so the data must be transferred during relatively short and continuously shrinking maintenance windows. After the data is extracted from the sources and while it is transformed, data cleansing rules must be applied to address data quality concerns.

Historically, information integration has been limited to batch processing during maintenance windows (e.g., on weekends). The frequency of performing information integration tasks limits the currency of the information that business users access through business intelligence (BI) applications. Today's business users need to make decisions and take actions much faster, so, more and more often, a need exists for *real-time* data transformation and integration. However, not all use cases require real-time data integration. The technology must support different latency mechanisms for different tasks.

In some cases, it is neither possible (e.g., due to business or federal policies) nor feasible to integrate the information by copying it into a common repository. The only integration option is *virtual and on-demand information integration*. In this scenario, only when it is requested is the information pulled from existing sources, integrated, and then returned, without being stored along the way.

IBM InfoSphere Change Data Capture is a high-performance, low-latency, real-time data integration solution that enables customers to easily sense and respond to relevant business data changes throughout the enterprise. With real-time data integration solutions, today's organizations are making better business decisions, running smoother operations, winning new customers and partners, and increasing their bottom line. They're using IBM InfoSphere Change Data Capture to:

- Load data warehouses in real time so they can make operational and tactical business decisions based on the latest information

- Dynamically route data, based on content, to various message queues to be consumed by one or more applications to ensure accurate and reliable data across the enterprise

- Populate real-time dashboards for on-demand analytics and business process management (BPM) to integrate information between mission-critical systems and Web applications so employees, customers, and partners have access to real-time information

- Consolidate financial data across systems in different regions, departments, or business units

- Improve the operational performance of systems that are adversely affected by shrinking nightly batch windows and expensive query and reporting functions

Information Reach

Many organizations are beginning to see their data warehouse as an incredible information asset that is not being leveraged to its fullest extent. It is not enough to have the right information—that information needs to be available to the decision-maker at the time of the decision! Most of the information required to make critical decisions is locked away in the corporate data warehouse. According to a Gartner Group study, less than 8% of corporate staff has access to information contained in their data warehouse.

The primary channel discussed in this book for delivering information is through BI or analytic applications. As noted earlier, business users who interact with such applications need access to information that often resides in disparate sources and requires integration and transformation. One of the remaining challenges is how to ensure that these applications do not establish yet another silo. Companies are coupling their operational systems with their decision systems to gain real competitive advantage by leveraging information. They are able to understand the facts of the decision before it is committed. Many other applications and business processes also need access to trusted information. How do we prevent each application from accessing, integrating, and transforming the data in different ways? How do we ensure that future and strategic information delivery channels do not yet again become inconsistent? The most effective way to couple these systems is via a web service.

Flexibility and Reuse are Driving SOA Adoption

- Reusable assets **reduces costs**

- Standardization creates **agility**

- Mix and reconfigure quickly **gaining flexibility**

- Transparent sources for **greater availability**

- Isolation from sources for better **stability**

- Single code set for **reduced redundancy**

- **Better security, and compliance** through single occurrence

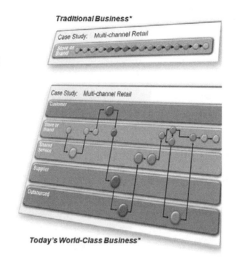

Figure 4.7: Operational applications are best delivered via web services

Figure 4.7 outlines the benefits of deploying analytics into operational applications as a web service. IBM InfoSphere Information Services Director, from Information Server, allows data integration processes to be published as reusable services in a service-oriented architecture (SOA). By delivering information as a service, InfoSphere Information Services Director ensures that applications and business processes are supported with accurate, consistent, and trusted business information while quickly meeting changing business requirements and reducing development cycles and IT expenditures. InfoSphere Information Services Director enables the delivery of data integration logic as a service; with development in minutes, without hand-coding, yet in a format that can be consumed in an SOA environment. This increases productivity of IT teams and lowers the cost of development efforts because business processes and information services can be reused and quickly developed to increase business agility and reduce development cycles.

The Information Services Director enables organizations to build simple web services that can deliver a small fact or enough data to show a trend. They are completely reusable, and can be the basic building block for building a more robust SOA environment. They can encapsulate federation or data integration or multiple other services. SOA breaks applications down into component services and then enables these services to be joined together as composite applications that can be rapidly constructed to meet the needs of changing business requirements. Using this approach, organizations are developing SOA information services to deliver the information to empower people and support the dynamic processes that drive their organizations toward business optimization. With the ability to understand, cleanse, transform, and deliver Integrated, Enterprise Data, and deliver all of this functionality as a service, SOA information services can provide trusted information directly to the application.

Certainly, the delivery of consistent, correct, and complete information is particularly important for master data (to be discussed in the next section). However, it is important for any data, whether master data or any other kind (e.g., unstructured information such as loan applications, financial data that includes key performance indicators). The challenge is how to guarantee *consistent delivery of trusted information* across a broad range of information.

Automating the Information Infrastructure

DataStage, a component of Information Server, can transform data of any complexity, from any source, into actionable information. IBM Information Server includes hundreds of prebuilt, metadata-driven transformation functions that can combine, restructure, and aggregate key data from its original application-centric form into entirely new contexts. Information can then be used in new ways to suit evolving business needs. By transforming and standardizing data so that it can be used in multiple business systems, IBM Information Server can automate and remove the complexity of integrating data from heterogeneous data sources, assure that information is in a form that is appropriate for its intended use, and provide critical information on the business at any time and to any authorized user.

Information Server can help create trusted integrated data and a data governance strategy to manage and administer your data. It can help build the trust and accuracy of data provided by processing all data through a unified process of discovery, cleansing, and transformation that results in trusted data. Gaining confidence in information is what drives decision-makers to bold, industry-changing decisions.

Unified Metadata Management and Deployment

An information integration approach needs to be built on a unified metadata infrastructure that enables shared understanding between the different user roles involved in a data integration project, including business, operational, and technical domains.

This common, managed infrastructure helps reduce development time and provides a persistent record that can improve confidence in information while helping to eliminate manual coordination and synchronization efforts.

One of the key business challenges introduced at the beginning of this chapter was the alignment of business and IT. Multiple user groups with a range of different roles from the business side as well as the IT side must be able to seamlessly and directly share information with each other across organizational boundaries and different roles. Streamlining collaboration among multiple, disparate users is critical to the success of any integration effort. Each module of Information Server uses the Metadata Workbench (Fig. 4.8) to preserve information from each step for subsequent reuse, while providing a valuable trail for traceability and auditability.

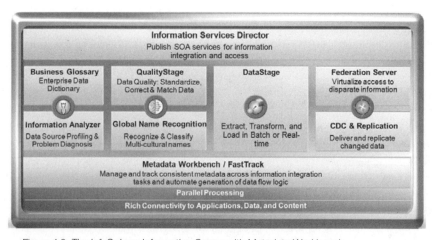

Figure 4.8: The InfoSphere Information Server with Metadata Workbench

Bringing Data Together for Analysis

The process of bringing historical data together for analysis is what is referred to as *data warehousing*. Organizations are focusing on modernizing their infrastructures and business practices to dramatically change their business. Their modernization strategies are focused on significant improvements in agility, efficiency, and cost optimization—in short, doing more with less—and changing business processes and market norms. Past decision systems are limited to reporting functionality, with little in the way of exploratory data analysis and in-process analytics. While some analysis is performed, the results are generally only available to less than 8% of the business.

New, intelligent organizations are finding new ways to use information by enabling the entire organization with the facts and information needed to confidently make informed decisions. They are using today's information to answer today's issues. Retailers are using information to upsell their customers offerings they are likely to buy at the time of purchase. Insurance companies are detecting and preventing fraud at the point of contact. Police departments are identifying suspects upon first arrival at a crime scene. Manufacturers are limiting inventory to better correspond with their forecasted orders. These are game-changing abilities, but they require information that can be trusted.

Enterprise Data Warehousing and Appliances

Gathering information and deriving value is what enterprise data warehousing has focused on for years. The problem has been that it was a long, costly, and difficult process. Data warehouse appliances have become popular because they can provide faster deployment—enabling business value much sooner. Appliances can also lower operating costs because the simplicity of an integrated solution reduces the effort and staffing required to maintain and manage the system. Appliances continue to be a hot topic in the marketplace and extend beyond data marts to enterprise data warehouse implementations. Today's data warehouses need to be tied into the operational systems in a bi-directional fashion, so that analysis from the warehouse feeds the day-to-day operations of the business. This is sometimes called *operational BI* and is described by IBM as an element of dynamic data warehousing. This blending of operational and data warehouse systems requires more sophisticated technology in order to enable better business decisions through things like immediate updates and analysis. In addition, focus is increasing on integrated analytics within the data warehouse. This acceleration of data into the warehouse means that there is no longer time to extract the data to remote tools and reload the results—decision-makers want today's answer today. Another trend is the increasing need to do analysis on unstructured data, which can make up over 80% of a company's information and which may not find its way into a traditional data warehouse. It is easy to see why many leading organizations are turning to a mission-critical enterprise data warehouse to build the "Intelligent Enterprise."

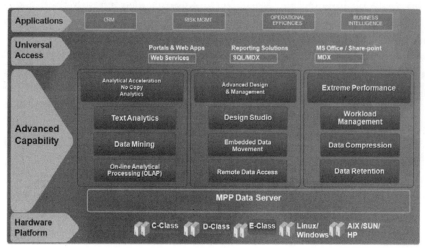

Figure 4.9: The InfoSphere Warehouse

The Intelligent Enterprise Powered by InfoSphere Warehouse

IBM comprehensively addresses all of the information management challenges just de-scribed with its InfoSphere Warehouse solution (Fig. 4.9). InfoSphere Warehouse is a ro-bust, flexible, and complete multipurpose environment that allows the intelligent enterprise to access, analyze, and act on highly current information—structured and un-structured, operational and transactional, current and historical. InfoSphere Warehouse enables companies to analyze and optimize all of their corporate performance manage-ment business processes. In this context, InfoSphere Warehouse can provide business us-ers with an integrated, state-of-the-art solution for planning, budgeting, forecasting, modeling, consolidation, and financial reporting. This integration of information from multiple sources provides businesses the capability of identifying their most profitable customers, products, and channels. In addition, new opportunities can be explored to cross-sell services, anticipate future needs, and devise marketing programs that offer well-aligned products and services to your customers. IBM InfoSphere Warehouse can operate on distributed platforms as well as on the mainframe environment.

Information Lifecycle Management of the Warehouse

Information lifecycle management is essentially the ability to monitor, analyze, and manage the lifecycle of applications, systems, and processes in the data warehouse environment. The ability to control and optimize this environment includes setting policies to optimize the use of system resources (CPU, memory, disk). By implementing a comprehensive lifecycle management system for the data warehouse, organizations not only can save on costs but also will have a system that can support a high-performance, dynamic warehousing environment.

Effective lifecycle management of the warehouse must include:

- Storage optimization:
  - » Minimizing storage and memory requirements while not impacting performance

- Performance management:
  - » Monitoring and analyzing the environment in order to optimize performance

- Data retention:
  - » Policy-based lifecycle management of data to reduce storage and retrieval costs

- Workload management:
  - » Manage and control computing resources to support varying workload requests

Master Data Management

Master data is core business information that is generally spread across multiple applications and locations, such as customer data and/or product data. Due to that fact that it is usually managed by multiple lines of business applications, it is usually not managed on an enterprise basis (e.g., banking customers of loans, customers of savings, and customers of credit cards). This can cause duplication, inaccuracies, and frustration for customers, suppliers, and others.

While creating an integrated view of master data in the data warehouse is one way to get a single version of the truth, it does little for the operational applications. The blended data from the data warehouse could be loaded into each operation systems, but because each system has its own business rules, the data could quickly become out of sync. What is needed is a system that can securely manage the information for all the applications.

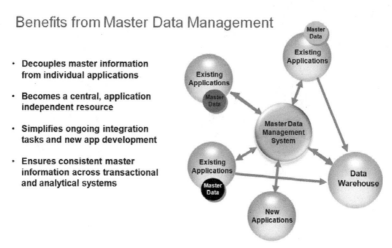

Figure 4.10: Master Data Management

Master Data Management (Fig. 4.10) is a solution that provides an industry-established model, a repository for storing data, and a large library of SOA web services to read, insert, update, and manage each of the fields of the master data.

Master data exists in the data warehouse as well as in the operational systems. For example, if John Jones goes into a retail location and makes a purchase, the John Jones information is master data, and his purchase information is operational data. After that purchase has been fulfilled, that purchase information becomes historical information and is migrated to the data warehouse (Fig. 4.11). The purchase information moved from operational to historical while the John Jones information remained master data.

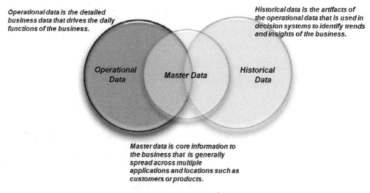

Figure 4.11: Master data versus operational and historical data

Master data management (MDM) builds on the information integration foundation and establishes trusted information or the core master data entities, ensuring the consistency of the most important business entities across business performance management applications and the enterprise.

The top reasons that organizations are deploying an MDM solution include:

- Cost reduction

- Cost avoidance

- Improved insights, relationships, and retention

- Increased revenue

- Enabling strategic initiatives

Data warehousing and MDM complement each other in developing enterprise data that can be leveraged for analysis and reporting. An MDM solution gathers and manages the common information for core business entities, such as customers, products, and locations. When combined with historical information in the data warehouse, master data can provide an in-depth view of a customer's behavior and preferences. Operational systems and applications also can use MDM systems to gain a single operational view of crucial data, which enables companies to verify the accuracy and consistency of information used in routine transactions, such as opening an account.

Creating consistency, correctness, and completeness of information is especially challenging for many businesses that do not take a holistic view of their organization and its information needs. Due to its nature, master data can be ubiquitous, existing in almost all systems. In addition, because these systems are often isolated and lack the proper integrity controls, their master data is often inconsistent, incorrect, and incomplete. Many organizations begin to take a closer look at master data as they attempt to comply with new regulations or merge multiple organizations. Gaining a single operational view of customers, products, or locations can become daunting without a MDM system.

Whether its building a data system to support analytics applications, reporting systems, or operational systems with master data, the one common thread is the requirement for user's confidence in the data. The need for information that is understandable, accurate, timely, and in context is what drives leaders in every market. A variety of tools and approaches are available for extracting, transforming, and loading data: The objective is to do it in a way that leaves users with the confidence to use that information to change the business—to decrease the costs, find new revenue, and change the playing field before the competition sees the opportunity.

5

The Information Agenda

To effectively compete in today's dynamic and challenging global economy, companies are increasingly recognizing the need to use information more effectively. However, while most companies already have strategies in place to guide their business processes and applications, the information needed to support these processes is not often shared across the organization, and most companies lack a cohesive strategy to get the most value from their information.

The Information Agenda provides a proven approach for helping companies turn their information into New Intelligence. Using the Information Agenda, these businesses become smarter through a more unified approach to using information to support business objectives and improve performance (Fig. 5.1).

How does an Information Agenda enable New Intelligence?

Information Agenda Deliverables:

- Get more value from information to support strategic imperatives
- Establish an information infrastructure to support future needs while leveraging existing investments
- Ensure information accuracy and protection when it is defined, accessed and updated in multiple places
- Deliver short-term value while progressing toward the longer-term vision

Realizing New Intelligence through an Information Agenda includes:

- Establishing an end-to-end vision and business-driven value case across the client organization
- Aligning people, process, and technology to leverage information as an enterprise asset
- Architecting technology and leveraging existing information assets for speed and flexibility
- Accelerating information intensive projects aligned with business strategy to speed both short and long-term returns on investment

---

Figure 5.1: The Information Agenda enables New Intelligence

Figure 5.2 shows how an Information Agenda can be applied in various industries to drive new projects and benefits to the organization.

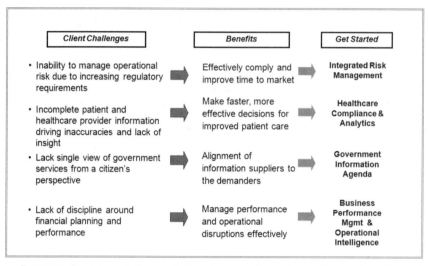

Figure 5.2: Complex and silo organizations have specific challenges that can be addressed by Information Agenda/New Intelligence solutions

Figure 5.3 illustrates the components of the Information Agenda, which organizations can use to deliver trusted, dynamic, enterprise information to drive and support New Intelligence applications.

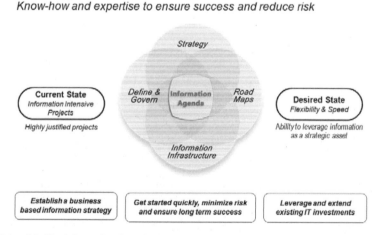

Figure 5.3: The Information Agenda framework

Information Strategy

The information strategy (Fig. 5.4) establishes those principles that will guide the organization's efforts to create and exploit information to support its goals, objectives, and initiatives. It provides an end-to-end vision for all components of the Information Agenda and is driven by the organization's business strategy and operating framework.

As part of the strategy exercise, the organization should identify its corporate objectives and initiatives for innovation and differentiation. The corporate goals, objectives, and initiatives are the vision and strategy identified by senior management that outline the direction the organization must take to maximize its inherent strengths and opportunities versus competitors. The information strategy should be revisited regularly to ensure it stays aligned with the organization's business strategy.

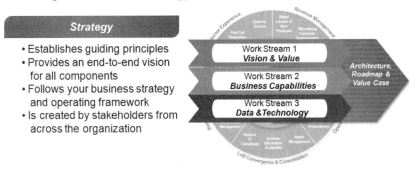

Figure 5.4: Purpose of the information strategy

Roadmaps

The information roadmaps (Fig. 5.5) identify the sequence of iterative projects and objectives that return tangible results. The roadmaps can be effective in enabling the CIO to set expectations and to identify the sources of any needed funding. They should address both short- and long-term opportunities, as well as provide a process for evaluating and tracking business benefits.

An Information Agenda Roadmap
Leveraging Your Business Intelligence / Performance Management Foundation
and Moving Towards the Future

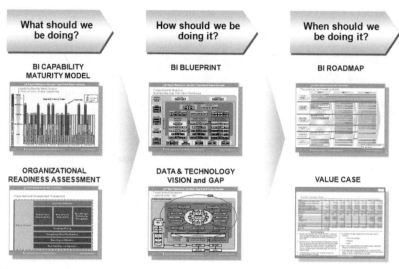

Figure 5.5: Information roadmaps

Information Infrastructure

To manage information as a strategic asset over time, companies must commit to an enterprise-level information infrastructure (Fig. 5.6). Narrow, application-specific architectures result in significant operational inefficiencies, unacceptable turnaround on projects, and the continued proliferation of multiple copies of data and content. Within the context of an Information Agenda, an enterprise information infrastructure framework identifies the technology required to integrate current investments with future technologies, helping to optimize return on investment.

Information Infrastructure

An enterprise-level information infrastructure can help you:

- *Manage information over its lifetime*
- *Use information as part of business processes*
- *Establish and maintain an accurate, trusted view of information*
- *Plan, understand, and optimize business performance*

Solution View and Architecture

Figure 5.6: An enterprise-level information infrastructure is a crucial success factor for managing information as a strategic asset over time

Information Governance

Once you have your objectives aligned, roadmaps defined, and your enterprise information infrastructure in place, management becomes the key to using the Information Agenda to sustain the value of information over time. Information, like any other corporate asset, must be managed. This management—which we call *information governance*—can enhance the quality, availability, and integrity of a company's information by fostering cross-organizational collaboration and policy-making (Fig. 5.7).

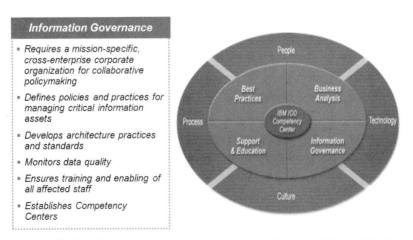

Information Governance

- *Requires a mission-specific, cross-enterprise corporate organization for collaborative policymaking*
- *Defines policies and practices for managing critical information assets*
- *Develops architecture practices and standards*
- *Monitors data quality*
- *Ensures training and enabling of all affected staff*
- *Establishes Competency Centers*

Figure 5.7: Effective information governance can enhance quality, availability, and integrity of enterprise information

Although it is sometimes challenging for the CIO and line-of-business managers to work together to establish information governance standards, the importance of this part of the Information Agenda should not be underestimated. Robust information governance is necessary for an organization to comply with external regulations more quickly and more completely. Information governance can help unlock the financial advantages that are driven by improved data quality, management processes, and accountability. Business performance can also be improved as a result of information governance, via common definitions and processes that drive effective strategy development, execution, tracking, and management.

Turning Vision into Reality

CIOs seeking to develop and implement an effective, business-aligned Information Agenda for the delivery of trusted information are going to need the assistance of their line-of-business colleagues. It is important, therefore, that CIOs obtain an executive sponsor—such as the board of directors, the CEO, or the CFO—who can position the Information Agenda as a strategic corporate initiative. This endorsement will help the CIO enlist line-of-business and other colleagues who are needed to participate in the development process and whose support will be critical to the success of implementation.

With strong executive sponsorship and a team of committed colleagues, CIOs can begin the accelerated path to an Information Agenda. To build its plan, the organization will need to go through several stages:

1. Vision lock

2. Business strategy and drivers review

3. Baseline assessment for maturity and capabilities

4. Future state development, opportunity identification, and prioritization

5. Integrated roadmap development and implementation planning

6. Kick-start project

These stages provide an accelerated, structured, and modular approach to defining, enhancing, justifying, and executing the Information Agenda. The stages are designed to align business and IT facets that impact the information agenda and to provide specific deliverables, including the following:

- Industry case studies

- Business value assessment

- Architectural readiness assessment

- Solution architecture

- Integrated project roadmap

- Software and services assets

In Conclusion

The business environment is fundamentally different—new economics, globalization, massive interconnections, and increased risk, coupled with an explosion of information. Business leaders making crucial decisions every day sense that they are operating with major blind spots, precisely at a point in time when margins for error have been reduced to nearly nothing, where costs have to be taken out of the system, and the velocity of decision-making is increasing exponentially. Intuition and gut-feel fueled mostly by personal experience are no longer sufficient.

A fundamental shift toward New Intelligence, a smarter, fact-based enterprise is essential—and possible—based on the broad application of advanced analytics to a far richer, integrated set of information. Companies can make this a reality by bringing together foundational business intelligence and performance management with advanced analytics, predictive modeling, world-class software solutions, and proven models that accelerate client time-to-value.

Business leaders must redefine their traditional scope of work to reflect the changed definitions of information, distance, speed, collaboration, control, and access. To operate in a smart world, they will have to imagine the data center without walls, be prepared to handle unknown future sources of information, identify insertion points for smart components, and consider how they present their company's reputation on a range of performance-based and socially responsible dimensions. Advances in systems integration, networking, and security will give rise to a smarter infrastructure that is simultaneously fast, and right.